National Clinical Guidelines for Stroke

Prepared by

The Intercollegiate Working Party for Stroke

Clinical Effectiveness & Evaluation Unit

ROYAL COLLEGE OF PHYSICIANS

March 2000

Comments on these guidelines should be sent to:

Penny Irwin, Stroke Project, Clinical Effectiveness and Evaluation Unit,
Royal College of Physicians, 11 St Andrews Place, London NW1 4LE

Tel: (020) 7935 1174, ext 335

Fax: (020) 7487 3988

Email: penny.irwin@rcplondon.ac.uk

Royal College of Physicians of London
11 St Andrews Place, London NW1 4LE

Registered Charity No 210508

Copyright © 2000 Royal College of Physicians of London

ISBN 1 86016 120 0

Typeset by Dan-Set Graphics, Telford, Shropshire

Printed in Great Britain by The Lavenham Press Ltd, Sudbury, Suffolk

The Intercollegiate Working Party for Stroke (1999)

Lead author

Professor Derick Wade, Professor in Neurological Disability, Rivermead Rehabilitation Centre, Oxford

Chair

Dr Anthony Rudd, Consultant Physician for Stroke, St Thomas' Hospital London and Associate Director (Stroke) Clinical Effectiveness & Evaluation Unit, Royal College of Physicians, London

Co-ordinator

Penny Irwin, Stroke Project, Clinical Effectiveness and Evaluation Unit, Royal College of Physicians

Association of British Neurologists

Dr Peter Humphrey, Consultant Neurologist, Walton Centre for Neurology & Neurosurgery, Liverpool

Association for Directors of Social Services

Mr Neil Walker, Director of Social Services, Dagenham, Essex

British Association of Social Workers

Ms Bridget Penhale, Senior Lecturer in Social Work, University of Hull

British Dietetic Association

Mrs Sue Bradley, Senior Dietitian, Birmingham Heartlands Hospital

British Geriatrics Society & British Association of Stroke Physicians

Dr Martin Dennis, Consultant in Stroke Medicine, Western General Hospital, Edinburgh and Chair of the British Association of Stroke Physicians

British Psychological Society

Dr Peter Knapp, Research Psychologist, Stroke Outcome Study, University of Leeds

Chartered Society of Physiotherapy

Mr Ralph Hammond, Professional Affairs Officer, Chartered Society of Physiotherapy, London

Ms Sheila Lennon, Lecturer in Physiotherapy, University of Ulster

Collaborative Stroke Audit and Research

Professor David Barer, Professor of Clinical Geriatric Medicine, Queen Elizabeth Hospital, Gateshead

College of Health

Dr Marcia Kelson, Research Fellow, College of Health, London

College of Occupational Therapists

Dr Caroline Ellis-Hill, School of Occupational & Physiotherapy, University of Southampton

Dr Marion Walker, Lecturer in Stroke Rehabilitation, Nottingham City Hospital

Different Strokes

Mr Donal O'Kelly, Director, Different Strokes

Faculty of Public Health

Dr Charles Wolfe, Reader in Public Health Medicine, Guy's, King's and St Thomas' Medical School, London

NHS Confederation

Ms Jenny Hawkes, South Cheshire Health Authority, Chester

Royal College of General Practitioners

Dr Colin Waine, General Practitioner, Bishop Auckland, Co. Durham

Royal College of Speech & Language Therapists

Ms Claire Gatehouse, Chief Speech & Language Therapist, Regional Rehabilitation Unit, Northwick Park Hospital

Royal College of Nursing

Dr Karen Waters, Professor of Nursing, University of Manchester

Ms Sally Davies, RCN Rehabilitation Forum and Rivermead Rehabilitation Centre, Oxford

Royal College of Physicians

Dr Patrick Gompertz, Consultant Physician, Royal London Hospital

Dr Miriam Chellingsworth, Consultant Physician, and Committee of Rehabilitation Medicine

Royal College of Psychiatrists

Dr Allan House, Professor in Psychiatry, University of Leeds

Society for Research in Rehabilitation

Professor Derick Wade, Professor in Neurological Disability, Rivermead Rehabilitation Centre, Oxford

Stroke Association

Professor Walter Holland, Chair of Research & Development, Stroke Association

For advice on qualitative research

Dr Pandora Pound, Research Fellow, Department of Public Health, Guy's, King's and St Thomas' Medical School, London

Continence Sub-Group

Professor Mark Castleden, Geriatrician, Specialist in Incontinence Management, Leicester General Hospital

Ms Hilary Dufferin, Continence Nurse, Specialist, Leicester General Hospital

Ms Katy Brittain, Sociologist studying the impact of incontinence on patients and carers, Leicester University

Ms Christine Norton, Nurse Specialist in Management of Faecal Incontinence, Northwick Park Hospital

Dr James Barrett, Geriatrician, Specialist in Faecal Incontinence, Clatterbridge Hospital, Wirrall

Ms Mary White, Continence Nurse Specialist, RCN Continence Forum

Contents

SERVICE EVALUATION

TABLES OF EVIDENCE

REFERENCES

APPENDICES

INDEX

How to use these guidelines

These guidelines cover the management of stroke, excluding primary prevention and subarachnoid haemorrhage. In order fully to understand the document all users should read sections 1 to 5. These explain the context of the guidelines, the way the strength of evidence is displayed, and the recommended guidelines for the overall organisation of a stroke service.

Thereafter the guidelines are laid out in similar format for each topic covered. Each section contains the context, the guideline, key references, with a statement on the quality of the evidence, where this may need further explanation. Areas for which local guidelines should be developed are also given.

Further evidence in relation to each section is given in the Tables of Evidence (pages 79 *et seq*).

Users wishing to find guidelines on a particular topic can look on the contents page or index, but are reminded that guidelines in other sections may also be relevant.

Background and development of the National Clinical Guidelines for Stroke

The guidelines were developed by the Intercollegiate Working Party for Stroke, co-ordinated by the Clinical Effectiveness and Evaluation Unit (CEEU) of the Royal College of Physicians in London. Funding was provided by the Department of Health for the guideline development but the working party was independent of the Department.

The members of the working party, listed at the beginning, were selected to give wide representation from all professions, to include representatives from social services and health purchasers, and also to represent the views of patients and their families. Members were required to liaise continually with their own professional bodies and with others as they felt appropriate. Most members had a longstanding personal interest and expertise in the field of stroke management.

Information to support the guidelines was obtained in numerous ways. Many publications, reports and other guidelines were used; the main author of the epidemiologically based Health Needs Assessment for Acute Cerebrovascular Disease was also the principal author of these guidelines; and members of the working party brought their own expertise and information from their organisations and professional bodies.

The literature review was led by the principal author with major contributions from the other members of the working party and their respective professional bodies. It consisted of systematic searching of available computerised databases: Medline 1966–, AMED 1985–, CINAHL 1982–, Embase 1988–. The Cochrane Collaboration database was used extensively, and other national guidelines were reviewed eg Agency for Health Care Policy and Research 1995 and Scottish Intercollegiate Guidelines Network 1997–8.

We have not attempted to use or give uniform, specific, defined search strategies, although such strategies are available, because the guidelines cover a great variety of topics. Individuals undertaking searches used their initiative to obtain the necessary information. Hand-searching of the literature was not undertaken, given the huge number of journals needing to be searched. However the Cochrane database of trials was used, and this includes information from hand-searched journals.

There was extensive and helpful peer review, including: discussion within different professional bodies; inviting specified experts to review the document; and dissemination to any person or group interested enough to review it. However, the quality of evidence was not evaluated by any formal procedure, because this would have been impractical for each guideline, given the wide range of topics covered.

Selection of articles for inclusion was based on the following principles. Where evidence specifically relating to stroke was available, this alone was used. In many areas the limited research available is less specific but is relevant, so some studies include patients with other, usually neurological, diseases.

Where evidence from meta-analyses or randomised controlled trials (RCTs) was available, this was used. Where there was limited or no evidence from RCTs, then evidence from observational group studies or small-group studies was used. In general, evidence from single-case studies was not used, primarily because it is usually difficult to draw general conclusions from them.

All guidelines were discussed and eventually agreed by all members of the working party. In general there were few areas of dissent but, where there was significant disagreement, experts outside the working party were consulted before final agreement was reached.

The first draft of the document was written by one person, following the literature review, and using further information and material provided by members of the working party. There was then a reiterative process as members reviewed the document, consulted with colleagues and professional bodies, and sought further evidence to modify, add to or subtract from recommendations. There were two rounds of formal peer review. The list of reviewers is reported in Appendix 1.

Although implementation of these guidelines may have cost implications, this document does not undertake a cost benefit analysis. Very few of the studies used to inform this document included cost benefit analysis or any consideration of costs. In addition, it was beyond the remit of this working party to undertake the large amount of economic evaluation required within the budget and time-scale given. Nonetheless we recognise that some guidelines do have significant resource implications, and have suggested that this needs to be considered locally.

Throughout this document the strength of the evidence supporting each guideline has been given, both using standard levels (Table 1.1) and descriptively.

As will be obvious from the document, there are many important areas of daily clinical practice without relevant evidence to guide them. Consequently we hope that all clinicians will consider participating in randomised trials being undertaken. Lists of research projects being undertaken are available from various sources (see Appendix 2).

Whilst the importance of research evidence to support guidelines for clinical practice is well recognised, the role of patients' and carers' opinions is less so. For the development of these guidelines the opinions and experiences of stroke patients and their carers were obtained through focus groups conducted by the College of Health. The findings, which were an integral part of the guidelines' development process, have been reported in Kelson et al 1998; and the recommendations from the report are given at the end of Section 1.

Utility review was conducted in a stratified sample of 40 trusts who had participated in the National Sentinel Audit of Stroke in 1998, and at least 20 volunteer sites, to identify how useful the guidelines would be in routine clinical practice. The results of this review are available from the CEEU. These showed widespread approval and enthusiasm for the publication of the guidelines. Many centres wanted to use them as the basis for local guidelines.

It must be recognised that research evidence changes continuously. The Intercollegiate Working Party for Stroke, funded by the CEEU at the Royal College of Physicians, London will be reviewing the evidence on an on-going basis. Any major changes to the guidelines, required as a result of changing evidence, will be made on the Royal College of Physicians website version, www.rcplondon.ac.uk.

Introduction

1 Introduction

1.1 Scope of the guidelines

These National Clinical Guidelines for Stroke cover the management of patients with acute stroke from onset, through rehabilitation, to the longer term. It is now proven beyond doubt that patients managed by a specialist co-ordinated stroke team in a stroke unit have lower mortality and morbidity (Stroke Unit Trialists' Collaboration 1998).

One major stimulus to develop these guidelines was the burden of stroke on the National Health Service, constituting over 4% of NHS expenditure, the third highest cause of death in the UK and the biggest single cause of major disability. There was also concern that standards of service varied widely around the country, and that practice was often poor. This was confirmed by the Clinical Standards Advisory Group report (1998) and by the National Sentinel Audit of Stroke, which showed that less than half of all trusts have stroke units and that patients are managed better within stroke units (Rudd et al 1999).

The challenge facing the NHS, social services and housing authorities is to translate known best practice into actual practice. These National Clinical Guidelines for Stroke are one method for improving stroke care nationally.

1.2 Purpose of the guidelines

The aim is to provide clinicians and managers with explicit statements, where evidence is available, on the best way to manage specific problems. Local services will need to add detail; the nature of that detail is indicated in each section.

These guidelines are directed primarily at practising clinicians involved in the diagnosis and management of patients with stroke. Their aim is to help the clinicians make the best decisions for each patient, using the evidence currently available. They are centred on the more common clinical problems faced in day-to-day practice, and are intended to be used by all professions, in all settings and at all points in the management of the patient following stroke.

The guidelines will also inform health purchasers and other agencies that may become involved with people who have had a stroke, for example when assessing needs and planning services. It may be relevant to national initiatives such as the National Service Framework for Older People and health improvement programmes. A version of the guidelines written especially for patients and their families will also be available.

The guidelines are concerned with the management of patients who present with a new clinical event that might be stroke. Their focus is the stroke itself, using the World Health Organisation (1978) definition:

> *a clinical syndrome typified by rapidly developing signs of focal or global disturbance of cerebral functions, lasting more than 24 hours or leading to death, with no apparent causes other than of vascular origin.*

The guidelines do not cover closely related general matters such as the control of hypertension or management of complications such as chest infection. Furthermore, they do not cover the management of subarachnoid haemorrhage.

1.3 Organisation of the guidelines

The principles underlying the guidelines are that they should:

- address issues in stroke management that are important;

- draw upon published evidence wherever possible;

- indicate areas of uncertainty or controversy;

- be useful and usable.

Stroke management is complex, so these guidelines necessarily cover many aspects of care. It is unlikely that any individual person or profession will wish to use or know them all, but each person does need to have some idea about their role in the whole team effort.

Organisation of the guidelines in a way that makes them usable (ie short and to the point), useful (ie covering all the many clinical problems faced on a daily basis) and valid (ie providing the reader with enough information to trust them) has been difficult. There is much available evidence, but there are also many important areas where no evidence is available and yet guidance is needed.

The organisation of this document is based on a comprehensive descriptive framework that covers all aspects of the subject. Within this framework the evidence published is often pertinent to several areas. However, we have tried to minimise duplication of evidence, and to cross-refer if necessary.

Section 2 gives the terminology and framework used throughout the remainder of the guidelines. Sections 3–5, on service provision, cover aspects of the overall organisation of stroke care and the general approach to stroke management, reflecting its importance and the strength of evidence available. The guideline starts with a general statement on organisation in any unit, and then considers some specific aspects of organisation, moving from the general towards the specific and culminating in general advice concerning the involvement of families and carers.

Thereafter Sections 6–11, on clinical care, are based on the themes of:

- **level of illness**. The model used is the revised version of the World Health Organisation's International Classification of Impairments, Disabilities and Handicaps (described in Section 2);

- **time post-onset**. Three main times are identified: early (approximately the first week); middle (up to 6 months); late (thereafter);

- **management process**. Three main processes are identified: assessment (including medical diagnosis); care (maintaining life, safety and comfort; otherwise known as support); and treatment (any intervention presumed to effect a change).

It is important to note that the evidence relating to specific individual interventions, usually drugs or surgery, is generally stronger, because it is methodologically easier to study such interventions in contrast to investigating multifaceted interventions over longer times. This does not necessarily mean that interventions with so-called strong evidence are more important than those where the evidence is weak.

1.4 Format

For each topic there is a consistent format:

- A short introduction, setting the scene.

- The guidelines, accompanied by grade of recommendation.

- One or two selected key references to the evidence supporting each guideline are given, with level of evidence, and reference is made to any tables giving the full range of evidence. The tables of evidence (page 77 onwards) contain details of the salient research studies.

- Areas where local guidelines may be considered.

Relevant quotes of patients and carers from the focus groups conducted to inform the guidelines (Kelson et al 1998) are given throughout. Whilst these are not standard evidence they provide important insights to the human element of these guidelines.

Each guideline recommendation is accompanied by a letter (A, B or C) to indicate the strength of recommendation supporting it. Besides the evidence, the level of evidence is demonstrated by a number (I to IV) indicating its provenance. Table 1.1 shows the meaning of each; these levels and grades are used because they are currently the preferred way of indicating the strength of any guideline or supporting evidence. The 'Evidence' paragraphs also give an indication of the nature and extent of the supporting evidence, together with some references. Lastly, for each topic, there is a table or group of tables giving further details of the main studies.

The working party found that these recommended grades and levels of evidence were not well suited to these guidelines. They fail to acknowledge or take into account: the clinical importance of the topic or the clinical relevance of the study finding; the size and power of studies, simply rating them on their design; and the credibility of the study and the findings. The strict relationship between grade of recommendation and level of evidence was also considered inappropriate, in part because it rendered one redundant.

Many areas of important clinical practice did not have evidence available to construct guidelines. We have therefore chosen to use consensus statements from this and other working parties, and to advise on local guideline development.

Table 1.1 Guideline strength: level of evidence and grade of recommendation

Level of evidence	Type of evidence	Grade of recommendation
Ia	Meta-analysis of randomised controlled trials (RCTs)	**A**
Ib	At lease one RCT	**A**
IIa	At least one well designed, controlled study but without randomisation	**B**
IIb	At least one well designed, quasi-experimental study	**B**
III	At least one well designed, non-experimental descriptive study (eg comparative studies, correlation studies, case studies)	**B**
IV	Expert committee reports, opinions and/or experience of respected authorities	**C**

1.5 Context and use

The guidelines should be taken as statements to inform the clinician, not as rigid rules. Guidelines cannot cover every eventuality; new evidence is published every day. Feedback is most welcome, because these guidelines will be kept up-to-date on a regular basis, reflecting comments from practising clinicians and the development of new evidence, if funding is provided.

The working party has deliberately chosen not to specify individual professions unless absolutely necessary. Stroke management requires a multidisciplinary team and allocation of duties between staff may vary in different places. Consequently the term 'clinician' has been used to include any healthcare professional (including social workers).

The guidelines may be used to inform decisions on standards of good practice, and indeed are closely linked to the Royal College of Physicians audit package on stroke services (Intercollegiate Working Party for Stroke, 2000). However, it would be inappropriate simply to use the guidelines as standards in themselves without ensuring that the evidence has been brought up-to-date and without discussing how relevant and appropriate they are in the context proposed.

These guidelines relate particularly to the management of stroke; they do not specifically cover areas of routine good clinical practice such as courtesy, managing associated illness, and making notes. It is assumed that they will be used within the context of the services available in the UK, and that clinicians and others will be operating within professionally recognised standards of practice.

The reader is reminded that practice needs to be set within the context of the current legal framework governing the provision of services, eg that applicable to community care or to social services case management. These guidelines do not intend to overrule such regulations, but to improve them in practice.

1.6 Recommendations from the report on patient and carer focus groups conducted by the College of Health

The views of patients and carers regarding their management after stroke were sought through focus groups organised by the College of Health. The report on these groups (Kelson et al 1998) highlighted many deficiencies in current services and made recommendations for the guidelines. These are given below. Patients' comments from the report (using the original language) are also quoted throughout the document.

a Guidelines and service development

The views of both patients and carers can and should be obtained to complement other forms of evidence in developing clinical guidelines. Priorities of patients and carers may differ from those of professionals. This has application for other chronic conditions beyond the field of stroke, and for other initiatives, for example National Service Frameworks.

b Access to quality services

Patients and their carers want timely access to quality services appropriate to their needs. The focus groups revealed various problems in accessing diagnostic, treatment, rehabilitation and support services. After access, participants also highlighted deficiencies in the quality of some services. Guideline developers should consider using patient quotes as one method for drawing attention to patient concerns about access to and quality of services.

See Section 3 and throughout

c Knowledgeable staff

Patients and carers want to be looked after by knowledgeable staff who understand the full range of their needs after a stroke. These include communication, personal care, treatment, therapy, support and information needs. Staff knowledge of these could be developed by training for all clinical and support staff involved in caring for stroke patients, regardless of where they are providing that care (eg on a dedicated stroke unit, a general medical ward or in the patient's home).

See Section 3

d Shared decision-making

The diagnosis and management plan are not always explained in a manner that patients and carers can comprehend and recall. Patients want to be treated as responsible adults, and carers want to know precisely what is being done or planned for their relative.

This could be helped by

- a written plan of care for the time in hospital and post-discharge;
- a written information pack including advice on local statutory and voluntary services available in the community;
- a clear indication as to what services are to be offered post-discharge, and advance warning of when services are to end;

> ▶ arrangements for post-stroke monitoring of patients, possibly by therapists or a specialist nurse;

> ▶ arrangements for assessing the practical and emotional needs of the carers and families of stroke patients, recognising that these may vary over time.
>
> See sections 4, 5, 10, 11

e Information when at home

There are many uncertainties for patients and carers after a stroke. These are often further exacerbated by inadequate direction to appropriate information sources or by poor quality of the information that is accessed. Patient and carers need to be offered relevant user-friendly information at each stage of their care and to have access to contacts for further questions and problems that arise later.

This could be helped by

> ▶ a named contact (with telephone number) for further advice after discharge; the named person must have the authority to investigate and rectify problems brought to them;

> ▶ information packs for carers, specifically addressing carer information and support needs;

> ▶ patients not requiring admission to hospital should also have access to this information.
>
> See sections 3, 5, 10, 11

f Patient and carer versions of guidelines

Patients and carers should know what care they may expect. This could be helped by providing a patient/carer-friendly version of the guidelines and making this available on all healthcare premises.

See sections 3, 5, 10, 11

Patient versions of the guidelines are available

g Links with patient/carer organisations

At local level, links with patient and carer organisations with a specific interest in stroke care, eg the Stroke Association; Different Strokes; Action for Dysphasic Adults (Speakability), should be developed and strengthened. Trusts and primary care groups may be best placed to develop and strengthen these links. Additional resources may be needed to ensure continued input from patient and carer organisations. Future studies need to investigate the specific needs of younger stroke patients.

See sections 10, 11, 12

Service provision

2 Terminology and theoretical framework

One of the major factors impeding good stroke care is the lack of any widely accepted, easily understood framework with its attendant vocabulary and terminology. The lack of an agreed model for stroke care may adversely affect communication between members of a team, between different teams and different professions, between different organisations, and between commissioners and providers of health care.

Guidelines

a All clinicians should consider and discuss explicitly with their colleagues the terminology and framework they use, and each team should use a consistent framework (**C**)

b It is strongly recommended that the World Health Organisation's (WHO) International Classification of Impairments, Disabilities and Handicaps (ICIDH) terminology be used (**C**)

Evidence

There are two strong arguments supporting these guidelines. First, efficient and effective stroke management is best undertaken by a specialised team (Stroke Unit Trialists' Collaboration 1998). A team is a group of individuals who share common values and work towards common goals. This is only possible if members of the team use an agreed vocabulary. Second, it is common experience that differences in interpretation of commonly used words, and differences of opinion about the meaning of words, underlie many of the problems experienced in managing patients. Consequently there is strong logic supporting the need for an agreed terminology. A proposed terminology and framework is given in **Table 2.1**.

a The WHO ICIDH introduced a framework and terminology that is now widely accepted and used when discussing disabling conditions such as stroke (Wade 1996; Post et al 1999) (**IV**)

b The WHO ICIDH is being revised. The revised classification refers to 'activities' and 'participation' rather than 'disability' and 'handicap', but the latter two terms are used here as they are more familiar. The new version introduces the concept of 'contextual factors' which impact upon the manifestation of all diseases. Contextual factors are: social; physical; personal. The model emphasises that there are complex, dynamic relationships between all levels of illness themselves, and between the person and the contextual factors (**IV**)

Local guidelines

Local services will need to:

▶ specify the terminology used locally, or agree to use the suggested terminology and framework.

Table 2.1 Stroke management: clinical framework and terminology

ICIDH framework:

Illness of person	Synonym	Level of description
Pathology	Disease/diagnosis	Organ/organ system
Impairment	Symptoms/signs	Body
Activity (was *disability*)	Function/observed behaviour	Interaction of person and environment
Participation (was *handicap*)	Social positions/roles	Person in their social context

Contextual factors	Examples	Comment
Personal experiences	Previous illness	May affect response to this stroke
Physical environment	House, local shops	May affect need for equipment etc
Social environment	Laws, friends	May affect motivation, support etc

Rehabilitation:

Aims	Synonym	Comment
Maximise patient's social position and roles	Minimise handicap/maximise participation	Takes matters well outside health; personalises rehabilitation process
Maximise patient's sense of well-being (quality of life)	Minimise somatic and emotional pain, maximise satisfaction with life	Often involves education about reality of losses and helping patient to understand/come to to terms with losses
Minimise stress on and distress of the family	Provide emotional and practical help	Takes matters well outside health; also takes much effort and time unrelated to 'objective' losses

Processes	Explanation	Comment
Assessment	Collection and interpretation of data	Only as much as is needed to take action, setting goals and intervening
Setting goals	Considering both long-term aims and short-term methods	Should be multiprofessional goals as well as uniprofessional goals
Intervention		
Giving/organising care	Intervention needed to maintain life and safety	Major resource use, proportional to dependence/disability
Giving/organising treatment	Intervention presumed to affect process of change	Usually referred to as 'therapy'; not necessarily face-to-face interaction
Re-evaluation	Checking effects of intervention	Re-iterative until no further goals remain

Other terminology:

Term/word	Definition	Comment
Outcomes	Result of intervention (or disease course over time)	Depends upon level being monitored, but for service should be at level of disability
Measurement	Comparison of data against a standard or 'metric'	Quantifies data (NB Data still need interpretation)
Audit	Comparison of observed performance against agreed standards followed by change	With the aim to improve service quality on a continuing basis. Interpretation should take into account case-mix and context
Goals (in rehabilitation)	Any defined change in state over time and/or future state	Generic term, no implications as to level, time frame etc
Aims (in rehabilitation)	Long-term goals set	Usually refers to (social) situation after discharge
Objectives (in rehabilitation)	Medium-term goals set	Usually multiprofessional, in weeks/months, at level of disability
Targets (in rehabilitation)	Short-term, specific goals	Usually named person and set time/place

3 Service organisation

Each stroke patient leads clinicians down a unique pathway, identifying and resolving a host of different combinations of problems in each case. It is therefore difficult to give many guidelines that will apply to every patient. Efficient and effective management of patients depends upon a well organised, expert service that can respond to the particular needs of each individual patient. Consequently the organisation of stroke services must be considered at every level: health district; primary care group; hospital ward; and patients in their own homes or in residential care.

Three aspects of organisation are addressed in this Section:

▶ **the need for services specialising in stroke (3.1)**

▶ **the specific needs of younger people with stroke (3.2)**

▶ **the place where these services are delivered (3.3)**

Other aspects of organisation are covered later in these guidelines.

3.1 Specialist stroke services

Guidelines

a Every organisation involved in the care of stroke patients over the first 6 months should ensure that stroke patients are the responsibility of and are seen by services specialising in stroke and rehabilitation (**A**)

The stroke service should comprise:

i a geographically identified unit acting as a base, and as part of the inpatient service (**A**)

ii a co-ordinated multidisciplinary team (**A**)

iii staff with specialist expertise in stroke and rehabilitation (**A**)

iv educational programmes for staff, patients and carers (**A**)

v agreed protocols for common problems (**A**)

b Specialist stroke services can be delivered to patients, after the acute phase, equally effectively in hospital or in the community, provided that the patient can transfer from bed to chair before going home (**A**)

c   Specialist day hospital rehabilitation or specialist domiciliary rehabilitation can be offered to outpatients with equal effect (**A**)

d   Each district should conduct a needs assessment exercise to determine the level of service so that all stroke patients in the area have access to the same standards of care (**C**)

e   Patients not admitted to hospital should be seen by a specialist rehabilitation team that includes a specialist occupational therapist (**A**)

Evidence *(Tables 3.1–3.7 pp79–83)*

Most of the evidence comes from meta-analyses or multiple randomised controlled trials (RCTs), but some is secondarily derived from those studies. The main references for each guideline are:

a   Stroke Unit Trialists' Collaboration 1998. The evidence in support of this guideline is overwhelming, and achieving this guideline should be the highest priority of all clinicians and managers (**Ia**). Tables 3.1–3.7 contain most of the supporting evidence: for (i)–(iii) see Stroke Unit Trialists' Collaboration 1998 (**Ia**); (iv) Jones et al 1998 (**Ib**); (v) Naylor et al 1994 (**Ib**)

b   Table 3.3: Rudd et al 1997; Early Supported Discharge Trialists 1999 (**Ia**)

c   Table 3.4: Gladman et al 1993 (but see Dekker et al 1998); Forster et al 1999b. There are several studies investigating this; the cost-benefit equation is not fully investigated yet (**Ib**)

d   Consensus of working party; Clinical Standards Advisory Group report 1998 (**IV**)

e   Walker et al 1999 (**Ib**)

Local guidelines

All purchasers (primary health care groups, health authorities) and all providers (hospital services, community services etc) in a health district will need to discuss and agree:

1   which local providers are to be involved in a co-ordinated, specialised stroke management service;

2   who will be the lead clinician, to be responsible for all local stroke services in general, and the multidisciplinary team in particular;

3   if more than one provider, how they allocate responsibilities and who leads;

4   who will undertake a local needs assessment, and how;

5   where the service is to have its central base (ie where the 'stroke unit' is);

6   the balance between hospital services, day hospitals, and domiciliary services;

7   how services work together effectively;

8   how training and education is to be provided;

9   the actual numbers of specialist staff needed;

10 evidence-based protocols for common problems.

Patient's opinion: Everything is geared to stroke patients, it's a family atmosphere and it really is in my opinion a wonderful place for rehabilitation.

Carer's view: She was then moved, ... to ('x' hospital) which was supposedly a designated stroke unit. It was nothing of the sort in any way whatsoever. There were my wife and one other stroke patient in there, and the rest were all very elderly people who had to be found a bed whilst they were waiting to go into care.

Patient's opinion: Whoever decided that they would invent Lakeside should be given a knighthood because they are really the tops… she was stretchered in and she walked out seven months later… I have to add to the physio people… the occupational therapists there who were dramatic.

3.2 Younger people with stroke

Stroke is predominantly a disease of people aged over 65 years, but a significant number will be younger. This group of patients may not fit easily into standard services. Their medical needs may differ, with more emphasis on diagnosing the specific cause of the stroke. Their rehabilitation may require specific and specialised attention to work prospects and bringing up young children. Their prognosis and social needs may be different.

Patient's view: I think people who's had a stroke and they're still… working, I feel very sorry for them – they need all the help they can get … you've got no future – if you've got (no) job.

Patient's and carer's view: It affects the children a lot.

Guidelines

a   Specialist medical and rehabilitation services must recognise the particular medical, rehabilitation and social needs of younger patients with stroke, and must be provided in an environment suited to their personal needs (C)

Evidence

a   Younger patients, through their organisation Different Strokes, have expressed significant concerns about the services they received which did not make provision for their specific needs, such as returning to work or full-time education, caring for a young family, etc (Kelson et al 1998) (IV)

Local guidelines

These should state:

▶ how the specific clinical, rehabilitation and social needs of younger people with stroke are to be assessed and managed.

3.3 Acute care arrangements (hospital or home)

See also Section 6, and 10.1

Stroke causes most patients to become dependent at least for a few days. This dependency has a more-or-less rapid onset (minutes or hours), it varies in its nature and severity, and its prognosis over the first few days is unpredictable, with 25% of patients worsening significantly. Observational studies show that a significant proportion (10–45%) of patients are currently managed without hospital admission. In suitable circumstances, it may be feasible for patients to have their medical diagnosis and treatment undertaken without admission to hospital (eg by visits to hospital). This may change once specific acute medical treatment becomes available.

Guidelines

a Patients should only be managed at home if:

i the guidelines in section 6 can be adhered to (**C**)

ii care services are able to provide adequate and flexible support within 24 hours (**C**)

iii the services delivered at home are part of a specialist stroke service (**A**)

b Otherwise patients should be admitted to hospital for initial care and assessment (**A**)

c In hospital, care should be delivered in a ward or ward area with specialist expertise in stroke management (ie a stroke unit) (**A**)

Evidence (Table 3.6 p82)

The evidence is largely derivative. Evidence (see Section 3.1) shows that patients benefit from access to a specialist stroke service.

a (i)(ii) Consensus of working party (**IV**)

(iii) Wade et al 1985a,b; Langhorne et al 1999 (**Ia**)

b Table 3.1: Stroke Unit Trialists' Collaboration 1998; Langhorne et al 1999; the evidence in support of this guideline is overwhelming (**Ia**)

c See b (**Ia**)

Local guidelines

These should specify:

1   for patients managed at **home**:

  ▶   how acute medical diagnostic services are accessed for patients not admitted;

  ▶   what emergency home care services are available;

  ▶   their procedures (contact arrangements, etc);

  ▶   how community services gain access to specialist stroke services quickly and easily;

2   for patients admitted to **hospital**:

  ▶   which wards have the necessary expertise and organisation.

Patient's view: Having a Scottish accent – when I told the doctor my husband was ill [and] he was falling over. He said: 'Has he been drinking?'.

---

4 Approaches to rehabilitation

There is debate about the best overall clinical approach to rehabilitation of an individual patient, and there is significant variability in the specific interventions used. Given that each profession may consider the patient from a different perspective, an atmosphere of co-operation and consultation should be created. Because it is difficult to define and characterise approaches to rehabilitation, the evidence is difficult to find, and it is also difficult to interpret because the studies often investigate other factors. Some of the evidence used here is taken from studies in other chronic illnesses.

This section covers aspects of the organisation of rehabilitation:

- assessment procedures (4.1)

- teamwork (4.2)

- goal-setting (4.3)

- therapy approaches (4.4)

- intensity of treatment (4.5)

4.1 Use of assessments/measures

Assessment is central to the management of any disability. **Assessment** is used here to include both the collection of data and the interpretation of those data in order to inform a decision. **Measurement** is the comparison of some of the obtained data against some standard or 'metric', in order to give the data an absolute or relative meaning. Measurement and assessment are linked but not synonymous.

Guidelines

a   Clinicians should use assessments or measures appropriate to their needs (ie to help make a clinical decision) (C)

b   Where possible and available, clinicians should use assessments or measures that have been studied in terms of validity (appropriateness for the purpose) and reliability (extent of variability) (C)

c   Routine assessments should be minimised, and each considered critically (C)

d   Patients should be reassessed at appropriate intervals (C)

Evidence (Table 4.1 p83)

Although there is evidence that a structured assessment helps to identify problems (Wade 1998a; Wikander et al 1998), no specific evidence supports any particular guideline (**IV**)

Local guidelines

Local clinicians should:

1 agree which assessments are going to be used locally, in order to improve communication;

2 agree how frequently formal reassessment is going to occur;

3 not spend too much time or effort discussing and researching individual assessments (this can take years). It is important to allow some choice if there are strong views or equally good measures available.

4.2 Teamwork

The evidence strongly suggests that good stroke outcomes follow the involvement of clinicians working together as a team. A team is a group of individuals working together towards a single goal or set of goals. Given the high incidence of back injury, all team members handling patients must be taught safe and appropriate ways to handle patients, and should be taught to adopt a consistent approach for any single patient.

Guidelines

See Sections 5, 8.3, 9.1.2, 9.2

a All members of the healthcare team should work together with the patient and family, using an agreed therapeutic approach (**B**)

b Nurses should be an integral part of the rehabilitation team (**C**)

c All staff should be trained to place patients in positions to reduce the risk of complications such as contractures, respiratory complications and pressure sores (**B**)

d All staff should be trained in the recognition and basic management of communication and cognitive problems (**C**)

Evidence (Tables 3.1, 3.2, 8.4 pp79, 93–4)

a Consensus of working party; Stroke Unit Trialists' Collaboration 1998 (**III**)

b Consensus of working party (**IV**)

c   Carr & Kenney 1992; Lincoln et al 1996 (**III**)

d   Consensus of working party (**IV**)

Local guidelines

These need to specify:

1   the locally agreed therapeutic approaches for common situations;

2   training opportunities for all staff in moving and handling stroke patients.

4.3 Goal setting

One of the specific characteristics of rehabilitation is the setting of goals. However, the term is used loosely and practice varies greatly. Goal setting here refers to the identification of, and agreement on, a target which the patient, therapist or team will work towards over a specified period of time.

Guidelines

a   Goals should be meaningful, challenging but achievable (**B**), and there should be both short- and long-term goals (**C**)

b   Goal setting should involve the patient (**B**), and the family if appropriate (**C**)

c   Goals should be set at the team level as well as at the level of an individual clinician (**C**)

d   Judging progress against goals set (goal attainment scaling) may be helpful (**B**)

Evidence (Table 4.2 p84)

There is reasonable evidence for goal setting in rehabilitation (Wade 1998b), but most of it is not specific to stroke. Although goal setting is identified as good practice by specialists in stroke care (McGrath & Davies 1992; Rockwood et al 1993; McGrath et al 1995), the majority of studies are descriptive and based on small samples for other patient populations.

a   Bar-Eli et al 1994, 1997; VanVliet et al 1995 (**III**) Consensus of working party (**IV**)

b   Blair 1995; Blair et al 1996; Glasgow et al 1996 (**III**) Consensus of working party(**IV**)

c   Consensus of working party (**IV**)

d   Stolee et al 1992; Rockwood et al 1997 (**IIb**)

Local guidelines

Local groups will need to agree on:

1 terminology (which is very confusing in this area) (see Table 2.1);

2 documentation (eg as given in Wade 1999);

3 the possible other uses of goals (such as goal attainment scaling as a means of monitoring progress).

4.4 Underlying approach to therapy

All approaches focus on the modification of impairment and improvement in function within everyday activities. Differences in approaches centre around the type of stimuli used and/or the emphasis on task-specific practice and/or the principles of learning followed.

Guidelines

a Any of the current exercise therapies should be practised within a neurological framework to improve patient function (**A**)

Evidence (Table 4.3 p85)

So far there is no evidence to support the superiority of one approach over another, but research is accumulating to suggest that patients derive benefit from therapy focused on the management of disability.

a Basmajian et al 1987; Jongbloed et al 1989; Richards et al 1993; Nelson et al 1996; Dean & Shepherd 1997 (**Ib**)

Local guidelines

Local discussions should:

▸ achieve agreement on the approach to be used by all members of the team.

Patient who had a stroke in Austria: *They were there right away and then twice a day after that. They constantly showed you what you would be able to do for yourself eventually. But when I came back to England it took ten days before they even assessed me. I know now that all the literature says that the first few days or weeks are the most important but here, you're almost ignored.*

4.5 Intensity/duration of therapy

There is much debate about the amount of therapy that is needed. One important but unanswered question asks whether there is a minimum threshold, below which there is no benefit at all. Studies on well organised services show that it is rare for patients to receive more than 2 hours therapy each day.

Guidelines

a   Patients should see a therapist each working day if possible (**B**)

b   While they need therapy, patients should receive as much as can be given and they find tolerable (**A**)

c   Patients should be given as much opportunity as possible to practise skills (**A**)

Evidence (Table 4.4 p86)

There are few trials, and interpretation of most is confounded because services giving more therapy were usually also well organised and expert, in comparison with the control group.

a   Rapoport & Eerd 1989; a reasonably controlled but non-randomised study including non-stroke (**IIb**)

b   Kwakkel et al 1997, 1999; Lincoln et al 1999; Parry et al 1999. (**Ia**)

c   Smith et al 1981a; Langhorne et al 1996. (**1a**)

Local guidelines

These need to take into account local resources, and any relevant professional standards, and then to specify:

▸ the therapeutic input to be aimed for as a standard in a few common circumstances.

Carer's view: Help in hospital was good. I think we both found it very helpful and supportive when it first happened [although] half an hour per week [speech therapy] wasn't enough.

5 Carers and families

A stroke is a family illness. Initially, as in any other acute illness, relatives need information and support through the crisis, but it is different from many other acute illnesses, in that they will usually need long-term practical, emotional, social and financial support to cope with the many residual problems. The extent of the stress of caring for a disabled person and the factors influencing the nature and extent of stress have only recently been the subject of research. There is little research into ways of alleviating the distress. Consequently there is little evidence to help with guidelines.

Carer's view: Its completely affected the family, it devastates you.

Patient's view: We had to keep my son off school [to help care for the respondent and her dependent disabled husband]. My son eventually was excluded from the school and my friend went up and she said 'Look, I have told you and told you the woman has had a stroke'... they didn't want to know.

Patient's view: I never got anything at all. My [disabled] husband – nobody helped him.

Carer's view: I was in a full-time job which I'd had to give up when he was discharged from hospital. I don't know what my options were – he was totally dependent, you know, and you put him to bed and got him up and dressed, you washed him and everything like that.

Guidelines

a   The needs of the family to be given information, to be involved in taking decisions and making plans, and to be given support, must be considered from the outset (**C**)

b   Stroke services must be alert to the likely stress on carers, specifically recognising the stress associated with 'hidden' impairments such as cognitive loss, urinary incontinence, and irritability (**B**)

c   Information should be given to families on the nature of stroke and its manifestations, and on relevant local and national services (**A**)

d   Family support workers should be involved to help reduce carer distress (**A**)

Evidence *(Tables 5.1, 5.2, 11.2 pp87–8, 111)*

a   Consensus of working party; Wade et al 1986; Kelson et al 1998 (**IV**)

b   Anderson et al 1995; Dennis et al 1998; Pound et al 1998 (**IIb**)

c   Mant et al 1998 (**Ib**)

d   Dennis et al 1997 (Table 11.2) (**Ib**)

Local guidelines

These will need to:

1 define how to involve families from the outset;

2 ensure that information that is relevant, easily understood, and local, is readily available in suitable formats and languages;

3 describe how families are to be supported: who will do it, and how services are accessed.

Clinical care

6 Acute (specific, medical) diagnosis

This Section refers to the diagnosis of the pathology. Diagnosis relevant to secondary prevention is discussed in Section 11.3. Accurate diagnosis is important because all medical and rehabilitation management is predicated on the diagnosis at the level of pathology (disease) being accurate.

In stroke management the primary need is to separate stroke (a vascular event) from other causes of rapid-onset neurological dysfunction. At present it is necessary to distinguish routinely only the pathological subtype of stroke if specific treatments are being considered. These guidelines do not specify where or how the diagnosis is confirmed. They do not specify hospital admission, though this may often be the only practical means.

These guidelines focus on patients presenting with an acute-onset neurological deficit that is suspected to be a new clinical acute cerebrovascular event (first stroke or recurrent stroke). They focus on the positive diagnosis of stroke. They do not consider subarachnoid haemorrhage in any detail. They are not intended to cover the whole diagnostic process, or the diagnosis of any alternative or associated diseases. They assume adequate diagnostic acumen and access to basic diagnostic facilities.

Guidelines

a   It should be recognised that 'stroke' is primarily a clinical diagnosis, and that the clinical diagnosis can be relied upon in most cases; care is needed in the young, if the history is uncertain, or if there are other unusual clinical features such as gradual progression over days, unexplained fever, severe headache or symptoms and signs of raised intracranial pressure (B)

b   The initial neurological assessment should allow localisation of the likely cerebral area affected (C)

c   Brain imaging should be undertaken to detect intracerebral or subarachnoid haemorrhage, and to exclude other causes of the stroke syndrome, in all patients within 48 hours of onset unless there are good clinical reasons for not doing so (C)

d   Brain imaging should be undertaken as a matter of urgency if: (B)

   ▸ there is a clinical deterioration in the patient's condition;

   ▸ subarachnoid haemorrhage is suspected;

   ▸ hydrocephalus secondary to intracerebral haemorrhage is suspected;

   ▸ trauma is suspected;

> ▶ the patient is on anticoagulant treatment, or has a known bleeding tendency;

> ▶ the diagnosis is in doubt because of other unusual features.

e   Brain imaging should always be undertaken before anticoagulant treatment is started (**C**)

f   The diagnosis should always be reviewed by an experienced clinician (neurologist, or physician with special interest) (**B**)

g   The patient's cardiovascular status must be reviewed (**C**)

h   Chest X-ray should not be undertaken as a routine investigation at admission unless symptoms specifically indicate it (**B**)

i   MRI scanning should only be considered when diagnostic confirmation of a stroke in the posterior fossa is needed (**C**)

Evidence *(Tables 6.1, 6.2 pp88–9)*

Little directed research has been undertaken on the process of diagnosis, and most data come incidentally from other studies. No research has evaluated critically the role of brain imaging.

a   Twomey 1978; von Arbin et al 1981; Sandercock et al 1985; Ferro et al 1998 (**III**)

b   Consensus of working party; Royal College of Physicians of Edinburgh 1998 (**IV**)

c   This is primarily a consensus guideline, drawing upon several published consensus statements, (eg Edinburgh statement (Royal College of Physicians of Edinburgh 1998) and Royal College of Radiologists (1998), and agreed by the working party (**IV**)

d   Sandercock et al 1985 (**III**)

e   Consensus of working party (**IV**)

f   Ricci et al 1991; Kothari et al 1995a,b; Martin et al 1997. (**III**)

g   Consensus of working party (**IV**)

h   Sagar et al 1996 (**IIa**)

i   Consensus of working party (**IV**)

Local guidelines

There is no evidence to guide doctors investigating patients after stroke, but the approach discussed by Warlow et al (1996) on page 224 seems appropriate.

It is likely that local services will wish to develop local guidelines for:

1   CT scanning (given resource implications);

2 which physicians or neurologists should formally review the diagnosis;

3 cardiovascular assessment;

4 use of MRI scanning, if available;

5 investigation of the underlying cause of stroke;

6 the 'routine' investigations to be used in every patient;

7 the secondary investigations to be used and when they should be used.

Carer's view: This is my one criticism that nobody recognised that as stroke … over the next 10 weeks he had a series of mini strokes which nobody else ever saw, but I was always with him … I felt that I wasn't being believed 'cos I was the only one who saw these, … We took him in for a brain scan … and discovered he'd had a lot of brain damage from all these little strokes.

---

7 Acute (medical/surgical) interventions

After diagnosis, specific interventions designed to limit or reverse the pathological process(es) must be considered. These guidelines focus on routine treatments for acute stroke, including intracerebral haemorrhage but excluding subarachnoid haemorrhage.

If the patient is found to have an incidental or associated disease (eg heart failure) this should be treated in its own right. If the patient is found to have a 'complication' of acute stroke (eg bronchopneumonia) this should be diagnosed and treated in its own right. These guidelines do not cover treatment of associated or incidental medical or surgical problems that may be present.

Guidelines

a Aspirin (300 mg) should be given as soon as possible after the onset of stroke symptoms if a diagnosis of haemorrhage is considered unlikely (**A**)

b No other drug treatment aimed at treatment of the stroke should be given unless as part of a randomised controlled trial (RCT) (**A**)

c Neurosurgical opinion should be sought for cases of hydrocephalus (**B**)

d Anticoagulation should be considered for all patients in atrial fibrillation, but not started until intracerebral haemorrhage has been excluded by brain imaging, and usually only after 14 days (**A**)

e Centrally acting drugs should be avoided if possible (**B**)

f In each hospital the neurologist or physician with special responsibility for stroke should review the Cochrane Collaboration regularly, and should be responsible for being aware of new developments in acute treatment (**C**)

g Thrombolytic treatment with tissue plasminogen activator (tPA) should only be given provided that it is administered within 3 hours of onset of stroke symptoms, that haemorrhage has been definitively excluded, and that the patient is in a specialist centre with appropriate experience and expertise (**A**) (**There is no license in the UK at the time of going to press**).

h Local policies should be agreed in relation to the early management of hypertension, hyperglycaemia, hydration and pyrexia (**C**)

Evidence *(Tables 7.1, 7.2 pp90–1)*

Meta-analyses have been undertaken for many drug interventions. For most drugs the evidence is simply too weak to recommend use at this point. Surgical interventions are not well researched, but there is no evidence to support **routine** surgical evacuation of intracerebral haemorrhage. The tables show the Cochrane Collaboration reviews and other studies. There are over 100 individual trials, and not all are referred to here.

a   International Stroke Trial Collaborative Group 1997; this is strongly supported by large trials, though the effect is relatively limited; Chinese Acute Stroke Trial 1997 (**Ia**)

b   See Table 7.1: Cochrane reviews; there is insufficient evidence to warrant the use of most drugs, and some can be considered detrimental (**Ia**)

c   Mathew et al 1995; Prasad & Shrivastava 1998 (**III**)

d   Stroke Prevention in Atrial Fibrillation Investigators 1996; Gubitz et al 1999. Few patients with atrial fibrillation have been included in trials of early anticoagulation after stroke. The benefits of early anticoagulation may be offset by the risks of haemorrhage, though these may be less for small strokes (**Ia**)

e   Goldstein, 1995. This study supports animal work (**IIa**)

f   Consensus of working party (**IV**)

g   Wardlaw et al 1996; Liu & Wardlaw 1998. The European license for tPA is expected in early 2000 (**Ia**)

h   Consensus of working party (**IV**)

Local guidelines

Local guidelines should specify details on:

1   who is the physician responsible for keeping up-to-date on acute stroke treatment;

2   how the Cochrane database is accessed by anyone freely;

3   aspirin use, and whether or when brain imaging should be undertaken;

4   anticoagulation (eg who will be responsible for monitoring);

5   neurosurgical referrals for intercerebral haemorrhage;

6   involvement in RCTs of new drugs;

7   acute management of common areas of clinical concern. Four are given below, with suggested guidance, but there is currently no evidence, so local clinicians should discuss their own guidelines:

   ▶   blood pressure should not be lowered in the first week unless there is accelerated hypertension or dissection, but existing antihypertensive medication should be continued;

- blood glucose should be controlled within normal limits;

- hydration should be maintained within normal plasma osmolality;

- pyrexia should be controlled with paracetamol, fan and treatment for the underlying cause.

8 Early disability assessment and management

Assessment of disability is a diagnostic process that should precede all further action in rehabilitation. It is as essential in management as is initial medical diagnosis. It is likely, but unproven, that one effective aspect of organised care is the use of an early structured assessment of the patient's disability and other relevant matters, eg social situation. The value of assessment itself has been the subject of some research, though not usually specifically related to stroke. The main questions, unanswered by formal research, are what areas of impairment, disability or social context should be assessed as routine early after stroke (rather than as part of an ongoing rehabilitation programme), and what methods should be used.

Although the evidence supports the use of specialist services as soon as possible, it is likely that in most places patients with stroke will first be managed in a ward or organisation that does not specialise in stroke.

These guidelines specifically apply to the admitting ward or organisation and cover:

- ▸ **multidisciplinary general assessment: rehabilitation referral (8.1)**

- ▸ **swallowing assessment: management of dysphagia and nutrition (8.2)**

- ▸ **prevention of complications (8.3)**

- ▸ **bowel and bladder management (8.4)**

8.1 Multidisciplinary general assessment: Rehabilitation referral

See also Section 4.1

There is no evidence to support particular selection criteria for more active rehabilitation or admission to a stroke unit. If anything, those with more severe stroke have been shown to have the most to gain from it (Stroke Unit Trialists' Collaboration 1998).

Guidelines

a A multidisciplinary assessment using a formal procedure or protocol should be undertaken and documented in the notes within 5 working days of admission (**A**). The protocol should include assessment of:

   i   consciousness level, using a validated clinical method, on admission (**C**);

   ii   swallowing, using a validated, clinical method, to be undertaken within 24 hours by appropriately trained personnel (**C**); see Guideline 8.2.a;

   iii the risk of developing pressure sores, undertaken on admission (**C**);

   iv   nutritional status, using a validated method, to be undertaken within 48 hours by appropriately trained personnel (**B**);

   v   cognitive impairment, using a validated clinical method, within 48 hours of regaining consciousness (**C**);

   vi   the patient's needs in relation to moving and handling, within 48 hours of admission (**C**).

b All patients should be referred to a specialist rehabilitation team as soon as possible, preferably within 7 days of admission (**C**)

c Healthcare workers should consider their knowledge, training, competence, health and physical capabilities before every manual handling procedure, taking into account the setting and the available equipment (**C**)

Evidence *(Tables 3.1, 4.1, 8.1 pp79, 83, 92)*

Much of the evidence does not relate specifically to stroke.

a   Stuck et al 1993; Wikander et al 1998. There is some evidence to support the value of assessment in rehabilitation, which emphasises the need both for multidisciplinary assessment and for ongoing intervention (Wade 1998a) (**Ib**) 1–3 (**IV**); 4. Reilly 1996 (**III**); 5–6 (**IV**)

b   Stroke Unit Trialists' Collaboration Group 1998. This evidence is very strong (see Section 3.1) in general, though not on the timing (**IV**)

c   Health & Safety Executive 1992; Chartered Society of Physiotherapy, College of Occupational Therapy, Royal College of Nursing, 1997 (**IV**)

Local guidelines

There should be local agreement on:

1   who will do assessments;

2   how they are contacted;

3   the protocol or procedures to be used;

4   who should be referred, to whom, how, and when.

Carer view on continuity of care received in the general ward situation: You're getting... early clinical decisions...then some on-going clinical decisions... then...rehabilitation decisions.... They should be in a stroke associated unit where you get focused attention... it saves time, it saves money, it saves beds (so) they can deal with more people who've got....God knows what else

---

8.2 Swallowing, feeding and nutrition: assessment and management of dysphagia and nutrition

Dysphagia, an abnormality in swallowing fluids or food, is common; it occurs in about 45% of all stroke patients admitted to hospital. It is associated with more severe strokes, and with worse outcome. The presence of aspiration may be associated with an increased risk of developing pneumonia after stroke.

Malnutrition is also common, being present in about 15% of all patients admitted to hospital, and increasing to about 30% over the first week. Malnutrition is associated with a worse outcome and a slower rate of recovery.

Guidelines

a   All patients should have their swallow assessed as soon as possible by appropriately trained personnel using a simple validated bedside testing protocol (**not** the gag reflex) (**B**)

b   Any patient with an abnormal swallow should be seen by a speech and language therapist who should assess further, and advise the patient and staff on safe swallow and consistency of diet and fluids (**A**)

c   Every patient should have his/her nutritional status screened by appropriately trained personnel using a valid nutritional screening method, within 48 hours of admission (**B**)

d   Nutritional support should be considered in any malnourished patient (**A**)

e   Percutaneous endoscopic gastrostomy (PEG) tubes (**A**) (or nasogastric tubes) should be considered where patients are unable to maintain adequate nutrition orally.

f   Every patient with nutritional problems, including dysphagia, which requires food of modified consistency, should be referred to a dietitian (**C**)

g   Patients' needs should be assessed for the most suitable posture and equipment to facilitate feeding (**C**)

Evidence (Tables 8.1, 8.2, 8.3 pp92–3)

The evidence includes randomised trials, but some of the guidelines are extrapolating quite far from the evidence.

a   DePippo et al 1992; Odderson et al 1995. There is much evidence supporting the validity of simple clinical testing of swallowing, voluntary cough and pharyngeal sensation. Testing the gag reflex is invalid as a test of swallow, and the role of videofluoroscopy is yet to be validated (**IIb**)

b   DePippo et al 1994. The benefits of full assessment and advice seem plausible, but the trial evidence is limited (**Ib**)

c   There is evidence of poor nutrition in patients with stroke, but no trial proof that identifying this affects outcome (but see Reilly 1996; and Lennard-Jones 1992) (**III**)

d   Potter et al 1998. A meta-analysis shows probable benefit of improving nutrition in malnourished patients, but not specifically for patients with stroke (**Ia**)

e   Norton et al 1996. The only RCT (small and possibly not typical stroke population) showed benefit for PEG. The evidence is weaker for nasogastric tubes (**Ib**)

f   Extrapolation from Davalos et al 1996; Gariballa et al 1998; Penman & Thomson 1998 (**IV**)

g   Consensus of working party (**IV**)

Local guidelines

Local guidelines may need to discuss:

1   the standardised initial assessment of swallowing, and the training of staff in its use;

2   the use of videofluoroscopy and PEG feeding, both areas with resource implications, little evidence, and major ethical implications;

3   how and when malnutrition should be diagnosed and treated;

4   the training of staff in the management of patients with swallowing problems.

Carers' views: My husband was having tube feeding … for weeks it was going on … and the only reason they gave that he was still on tube feeding was that they couldn't get a speech therapist to look at him.

When she came out of hospital D. was four and a half stone. Pathetic. Couldn't hold a spoon, couldn't do nothing.... Me and the boy [their son] got on with it as best we could.

8.3 Prevention of complications

8.3.1 Positioning

See also Section 4.2

Therapeutic positioning of stroke patients is a widely advocated strategy to discourage the development of abnormal tone, contractures, pain, skin breakdown, and respiratory complications. It is an important element in maximising the patient's functional gains and quality of life. This section should be read in conjunction with Section 4.2 on teamwork.

Guideline

a   Staff should position patients to minimise the risk of complications such as contractures, respiratory complications, shoulder pain and pressure sores (**C**)

Evidence (Tables 3.2, 8.4 pp79, 93–4)

There are few studies relating to positioning. Positioning improves with formal teaching. It has been observed that patients in stroke units are more likely to be in recommended positions.

a   Consensus of working party; Carr & Kenney 1992; Lincoln et al 1996; Jones et al 1998. (**IV**)

Local guidelines

These need to :

▶ specify locally agreed procedures for positioning.

8.3.2 Venous thromboembolism

Venous thromboembolism often occurs within the first week of a stroke, most often in immobile patients with paralysis of the leg, but its impact after stroke is still unclear. Studies using radiolabelled fibrinogen leg-scanning suggest that deep venous thrombosis (DVT) occurs in up to 50% of patients with hemiplegia but clinically apparent DVT probably occurs in fewer than 5%. Similarly, although autopsy series have identified pulmonary embolism (PE) in a large proportion of patients who die, clinically evident PE occurs in only 1–2% of patients.

Guidelines

a   Aspirin (75–300 mg daily) should be given (**A**)

b   Compression stockings should be applied in stroke patients with weak or paralysed legs (once the patient's peripheral circulation, sensation and the state of the skin have been assessed) (**A**)

c   Compression stockings should be full-length in patients with hemiparesis (**A**)

d   Mobilisation and optimal hydration should be maintained as far as possible from the outset (**C**)

e   Prophylactic anticoagulation should not be used routinely (**A**)

Evidence (Tables 8.4, 11.3 pp93–4, 111–3)

a   Antiplatelet Trialists Collaboration 1994; Chinese Acute Stroke Trial collaborative group 1997; International Stroke Trial Collaborative Group 1997; post hoc analyses show a reduced incidence of DVT in patients given aspirin (**Ib**)

b   Wells et al 1994. Compression stockings reduce the incidence of DVT peri-operatively by 68%, and may be helpful after stroke, though no large RCTs have evaluated their use in stroke (**Ib**)

c   Wells et al 1994. The stockings used in this trial were full-length (**Ib**)

d   Consensus of working party (**IV**)

e   Gubitz et al 1999. Anticoagulants reduce the incidence of venous thromboembolism but increase the risk of cerebral haemorrhage (**Ia**)

Local guidelines

These need to consider:

1   protocols for assessment of peripheral circulation and criteria for use of compression stockings;

2   protocol for early mobilisation;

3   protocols for hydration from stroke onset.

8.4 Bladder and bowel management

Most patients with moderate to severe stroke are incontinent at presentation, and many are discharged incontinent. Urinary and faecal incontinence are both common in the early stages. Bladder training may establish continence in hospital, but cannot always be sustained by carers at home. Incontinence is a major burden on carers once the patient is discharged home. Management of both bladder and bowel problems should be seen as an essential part of the patient's rehabilitation, as they can seriously hamper progress in other areas.

Guidelines

a   Units should have established assessment and management protocols for both urinary and faecal incontinence and constipation (**B**)

b   Continence services should cover both hospital and community, to provide continuity of care (**C**)

c   All qualified nurses should be able to assess incontinent patients, and know who to contact for support and advice (**C**)

d   There should be active bowel and bladder management from admission (**C**)

e   Catheters should be used only after full assessment, and as part of a planned catheter management plan using an agreed protocol (eg smallest size that functions) (**B**)

f   Further tests (urodynamics, anorectal physiology tests) should be considered when incontinence persists (**C**)

g   Incontinent patients should not be discharged until adequate arrangements for continence aids and services have been arranged at home and the carer has been adequately prepared (**C**)

h   In selecting equipment, factors to consider include ease of putting on, appearance, and comfort (**C**)

i   Sexual function should be considered, particularly the potential problems associated with an indwelling catheter (**C**)

Evidence *(Table 8.5 p94)*

The evidence to date relates more to general continence management, with little specific to stroke.

a   Royal College of Physicians 1995, 1998; Wikander et al 1998 (**III**)

b   Consensus of continence advisory group to working party (**IV**)

c   Consensus of continence advisory group to working party (**IV**)

d   Consensus of continence advisory group to working party; Gelber et al 1993; Wikander et al 1998 (**IV**)

e   Kennedy & Brocklehurst 1982; Kennedy et al 1983; Rigby 1998 and Winn 1998 provide guidance on catheter complications and management (**III**)

f   Consensus of continence advisory group to working party (**IV**)

g   Consensus of continence advisory group to working party (**IV**)

h   Consensus of continence advisory group; Shirran & Brazzelli 1999 (**IV**)

i   Consensus of continence advisory group to working party (**IV**)

Local guidelines

These need to cover:

1 a specialist continence advisory service available to all stroke patients;

2 assessment and management protocols for patients with urinary and faecal incontinence;

3 levels of specialist training in continence management for nurses involved in the care of stroke patients;

4 what incontinence equipment will be provided, by whom, and who will pay for it once the patient goes home;

5 how to maintain continence at home.

9 Rehabilitation interventions

This Section provides guidelines on the approach to some common clinical problems. The domains covered are:

- psychological impairments: mood and cognitive disorders (9.1)

- communication: dysphasia, dysarthria and dyspraxia (9.2)

- motor impairment and spasticity (9.3)

- sensory impairment and pain, including shoulder pain (9.4)

- drugs for impairment (9.5)

- gait (9.6)

- activities of daily living (9.7)

- equipment and adaptations (9.8)

Carer: I said to the nurse: 'Well I've heard about [the rehab ward] could he possibly go there?' And she said: 'Oh, I don't think [they] can do any more for your husband than we've done. And at that time he was walking with a frame and having great difficulties – he couldn't see properly, he couldn't speak properly, and his blood pressure... still wasn't stable.

9.1 Psychological impairment

9.1.1 Mood disturbance: depression, emotionalism and anxiety

Disturbance, both of mood itself and of the control of mood, is common after stroke. Diagnosis of the presence or absence of an abnormal mood state is difficult, particularly in the presence of speech disturbance. Diagnostic separation of different abnormalities is also difficult, especially as they may coexist. The presence of any one disturbance should lead to consideration of other types of mood disturbance. Treatments may include drugs or psychological therapy.

Symptoms suggestive of **depression** are common after stroke. Such symptoms include crying, feeling miserable or hopeless, lack of motivation, reduced appetite, reduced social activities, etc. Diagnosis of the symptoms can be difficult in the presence of the impairments caused by stroke.

Crying is not uncommon after stroke. If it appears to arise with minimal provocation the patient may be experiencing **emotionalism**, an impairment in the control of crying (and, more rarely, laughing).

Feelings of fear and worry are also common after stroke. **Anxiety** is an unpleasant, uncontrollable affect of fear or apprehension, accompanied by autonomic (physical) symptoms, such as breathlessness, palpitations and trembling. The specific causes of anxiety after stroke are not known but in general it may be provoked by situations, such as a fear of falling when transferring on to a toilet, or fear of meeting people, or it can be a generalised anxiety disorder not linked to any specific provocation. Anxiety varies in its severity and thereby its impact on function. Some people may cope with anxiety disorder by avoiding the provocation.

Guidelines

a   Patients should be given information, advice and the opportunity to talk about the impact of illness upon their lives (**B**)

b   Patients' psychosocial needs should be assessed (**C**)

c   Patients should be screened for depression and anxiety within the first month of stroke, and their mood kept under review. In those patients who can respond to it, a standardised questionnaire may be used for screening, but any clinical diagnosis should be confirmed by clinical interview (**C**)

d   Emotionalism after stroke should be confirmed by a few simple questions at clinical interview (**B**)

e   Any patient diagnosed with one form of mood disorder should be assessed for the others (**B**)

f   Patients with severe, persistent or troublesome tearfulness (emotionalism) should be given antidepressant drug treatment, monitoring the frequency of crying to check effectiveness (**A**)

g   Patients in whom a depressive disorder has been diagnosed should be considered for a trial of antidepressant medication (**A**)

h   Mood disorder that is causing persistent distress or worsening disability should be managed by or with advice from an experienced clinical psychologist or psychiatrist (**C**)

Evidence (Tables 9.1, 9.2 pp95–6)

There is much evidence on the prevalence of depressive symptoms after stroke, but it is difficult to use the available evidence to guide specific treatment. The primary difficulty is in deciding whether a specific intervention is needed to improve the mood state and, if so, what intervention.

a   Evans et al 1988 (Table 11.2); Pain & McLellan 1990 (Table 5.2) (**III**)

b   College of Health report (Kelson et al 1998) identified the widespread need for support. Consensus of working party (**IV**)

c   Consensus of working party (**IV**)

d   Allman et al 1992 (**III**)

e   Schultz et al 1997 (**III**)

f   Brown et al 1998; Andersen et al 1993 (**Ib**)

g   Lipsey et al 1984; Andersen et al 1994 (**Ib**)

h   Consensus of working party (**IV**)

Local guidelines

Local services will need to agree:

1   who will give expert clinical psychology and/or psychiatric input;

2   how to access the expert service;

3   standards in terms of response time etc.

Carers' views: We don't know what's going on in his brain. And now he's so emotional. He cries for little, little things. He just starts crying all the time.

There's no emotional back up, but it's all very clinical, you know... It's all to do with physiotherapy and speech but they forget the other side of it.

9.1.2 Cognitive impairment

Impaired cognition is common after stroke, and up to 25% of long-term survivors have such severe generalised impairment that they may be diagnosed as suffering dementia. Specific impairments seen (excluding aphasia) include visuospatial neglect, apraxia, impaired learning, reduced attention, and a host of more rare deficits. Their importance is that they may explain an otherwise inexplicable disability; for example, impaired attention, planning or visuospatial abilities may explain difficulty in dressing.

Guidelines

a   Every stroke rehabilitation service should have ready rapid access to expert neuropsychological expertise to assess patients (**C**)

b   Patients with persistent visual neglect or visual field defects should be offered specific retraining strategies (**A**)

Evidence (Table 9.3 p96)

a   Consensus of working party (**IV**)

b   Kerkhoff et al 1994; Kalra et al 1997 (**Ib**)

Local guidelines

These will need to:

▶ specify the expert local clinical psychologist and/or occupational therapist, and how they are to be contacted.

9.2 Communication: Dysphasia, dysarthria, and articulatory dyspraxia

Stroke can affect communication in different ways. The patient may have impaired motor speech production (dysarthria) resulting in unnatural or unintelligible speech; they may have impaired language skills (aphasia or dysphasia); or they may have impaired planning and execution of motor speech (articulatory dyspraxia). The patient may have subtle communication problems due to higher level language impairment associated with non-dominant hemisphere stroke. Untrained clinicians may misdiagnose the cause of abnormal communication. Accurate diagnosis is essential to guide and inform the team and the family. A speech and language therapist is the most competent person to assess a patient with abnormal communication.

Guidelines

a   Every patient with a dominant hemisphere stroke should be assessed for dysphasia using a reliable and valid method (**C**)

b   Every patient with difficulties in communication should be assessed fully by a speech and language therapist (SLT) (**B**)

c   If the patient has communication difficulties, the staff and relatives should be informed by the SLT of communication techniques appropriate to the impairment (**A**)

d   Where achievable goals can be identified, and continuing progress demonstrated, patients with communication difficulties should be offered appropriate treatment, with monitoring of progress (**A**)

e   Patients with specific communication difficulties should be assessed by a SLT as to their suitability for intensive speech and language therapy treatment which the trials suggest should be for a 4–8 week period (**B**)

f   For patients with long-term language difficulties, especially with reading, a period of reading retraining should be considered (**A**)

g Any patient with severe communication disability but reasonable cognition and language should be assessed for and provided with appropriate alternative or augmentative communication aids (C)

Evidence *(Table 9.4 p97)*

The table shows evidence for interventions currently evaluated for speech and language disorders: assessment; treatments by therapists or volunteers; drugs; and computers. There are many well designed single-case studies not included in the table; a list may be obtained from Action for Dysphasic Adults.

a Enderby et al 1998 (**IV**)

b David et al 1982. One of several studies suggesting a specific benefit from assessment (**IIb**)

c David et al 1982; Wertz et al 1986; Rice et al 1987; Lyon et al 1997 (**Ib**)

d Wertz et al 1986; Whurr et al 1992; Robey 1994, 1998; Greener et al 1999 (**Ib**)

e Brindley et al 1989; Poeck et al 1989; Mackenzie 1991 (**IIa**)

f Bruce & Howard 1987; Katz & Wertz 1997 (**Ib**)

g Consensus of working party (**IV**)

Local guidelines

These need to specify:

1 the methods to be used by appropriately trained practitioners to screen patients for, and with disordered communication;

2 the local options for routine and specialist or intensive treatments, including setting, the availability and flexibility of treatment packages, and how these services are accessed;

3 eligibility for, access to, and funding of communication aids; provision of training available for healthcare and related practitioners to enhance communication with patients with communication difficulties;

4 assessments and measures to be used by local speech and language therapists.

Carer's view: We're still hearing stories of patients not being washed, because....the nurses have said 'Do you want a wash?' and they've said 'No', but the patient didn't mean 'no', because [as] most people know with strokes, people say 'No' – and they mean 'yes'... and they don't stop to find out – so you do need a special sort of training.

Dysphasic patient's view: When F., who I live with, she'd come in... they would talk to her... they wouldn't look at me, they'd look at Flo and I [wanted] to say,... ''Scuse me, look at me, I'm here',... I was so annoyed..., people were talking away from me, not to me.

Dysphasic patients' views: It's not only speech that [helps] people like us, it's building up people's confidence, it's getting them to re-join life again...

...they're too gentle with us really and they should be tougher with us if they're going to improve your conversation, improve everything about you.

9.3 Motor impairment

9.3.1 Improving motor control: conventional

See also Sections 4.4 and 4.5

The aim of conventional therapeutic approaches is to increase physical independence through the facilitation of motor control and skill acquisition. There is strong evidence to support the effect of rehabilitation in terms of improved functional independence and reduced mortality. Currently there is little evidence to support the effects of therapy on improving motor control. There are additional techniques, such as biofeedback and functional electrical stimulation, that can be used as an adjunct to conventional therapy.

Guideline

a   A physiotherapist with expertise in neuro-disability should co-ordinate therapy to improve movement performance of patients with stroke (**C**)

Evidence

a   Association of Chartered Physiotherapists in Neurology (ACPIN) 1995 (**IV**)

Local guidelines

These need to specify:

1   the method used by appropriately trained practitioners to assess patients;

2   the local options for routine and specialist or intensive treatments, including setting, the availability and flexibility of treatment packages, and how these services are accessed;

3   provision of training available for healthcare and related practitioners to enhance patients' rehabilitation;

4   assessments and measures to be used by local physiotherapists.

Patient's view: For most people, to walk from there to there is... is hard, but with someone to help them and walk with them and taking the time with them is a necessity...

9.3.2 Improving motor control: biofeedback

During therapy, patients are usually given feedback on their performance as part of the retraining therapy. One method of enhancing feedback is to utilise technology to detect activity and to give feedback. This is biofeedback, and it is usually but not always based on electromyography (EMG).

Guidelines

a   Biofeedback systems should not be used on a routine basis (**A**)

b   Biofeedback should be considered as an addition to traditional therapy when retraining in standing balance (**A**)

Evidence (Table 9.5 pp98–9)

Biofeedback has usually been investigated as an adjunct to conventional therapy. It has been subject to several meta-analyses, with conflicting results.

a   Glanz et al 1995; Moreland et al 1998. The differences in conclusion in part reflect difference in study selection. The additional beneficial effects of biofeedback may be relatively limited. (**Ia**)

b   Dursun et al 1996; Sackley & Lincoln 1997 (**Ib**)

Local guidelines

As there is no evidence to support the use of biofeedback systems, no local guideline is needed unless a local team uses these systems, in which case they may wish to specify:

1   which patients are considered suitable;

2   how its benefit is to be judged for any patient trying it.

9.3.3 Improving motor control: functional electrical stimulation

Functional electrical stimulation (FES) is the use of direct electrical stimulation of muscle or peripheral nerve to cause movement. It has been proposed both as a means of improving muscle function (ie as treatment), and also as a way of replacing or augmenting weakened muscle function.

Guidelines

a   Functional electrical stimulation should not be used as a routine after stroke (**A**)

b   Individual patients should be considered for FES as an orthosis in certain circumstances, such as improving ankle dorsiflexion and gait performance (**A**)

Evidence *(Table 9.6 p100)*

a   Glanz et al 1995. Meta-analysis based on only a few studies, but does exclude a very large effect of FES. (**Ia**)

b   Burridge et al 1997 (**Ib**)

Local guidelines

As there is limited evidence to support the general use of FES, no local guideline is needed unless a local team uses or is buying it, in which case they may wish to specify:

1   which patients are considered suitable;

2   how its benefit is to be judged for any patient trying it.

9.3.4   Spasticity: assessment, therapy and use of drugs

Spasticity is a motor disorder characterised by a velocity-dependent increase in tonic stretch reflexes. Spasticity may lead to secondary complications such as muscle and joint contractures. Antispastic drugs, developed for use in spinal cord disease, are widely promoted, and botulinum toxin is now becoming available (see following section). In practice the management of spasticity may require several co-ordinated interventions, including physiotherapy and patient education.

Guidelines

After stroke, spasticity seen in the arm or leg:

a   should be treated **if** causing symptoms, using physical treatments and possibly drugs, though the functional benefit is uncertain (**B**)

b   should not limit the use of strength training (**C**)

Evidence *(Table 9.7 pp100–1)*

Despite being available for many years, and despite being widely promoted for and used in patients who have had a stroke, there is remarkably little evidence on the benefits or risks of using antispastic drugs. There is minimal evidence concerning physical treatments.

a   Ketel & Kolb 1984; Katrak et al 1992. There is reasonable evidence that drugs (and botulinum toxin; see later) reduce spasticity, but there is no evidence to support routine use in the absence of specific problems directly attributable to spasticity. (**IIa**)

b   Brown & Kautz 1998. A small trial supports a growing body of observational and physiological literature supporting this statement; Ada et al 1998. (**IV**)

Local guidelines

The main area for local guidelines relates to the use of botulinum toxin (see following section).

9.3.5 Spasticity: botulinum toxin

Botulinum toxin is a drug that has many potential advantages: it is generally safe, with minimal side effects, and it can be targeted to individual muscles. It has two potential disadvantages: it is expensive, and its effects reverse after 3 months (which in some cases could be an advantage).

Guidelines

In patients with disabling or symptomatically distressing spasticity:

a   injection of botulinum toxin should be considered for reducing tone and/or increasing the range of joint motion (A)

b   additional electro-stimulation should be considered for increasing the effectiveness of botulinum toxin (A)

Evidence *(Table 9.8 pp 101–2)*

In contrast to the situation with drugs or therapy, there is much more evidence relating to botulinum toxin (not all specific to stroke), presumably because it is expensive, it is effective, and it can be targeted without significant side effects.

a   Burbaud et al 1996; Simpson et al 1996; Hesse et al 1998. There are several trials in stroke and other diseases supporting the functional benefits as well as the reduction in spasticity. There is no evidence to guide selection of patients or to suggest that precise (EMG-guided) localisation is needed (Childers et al 1996) (**Ib**)

b   Hesse et al 1998. A small trial, but supported by animal experiments (**Ib**)

Local guidelines

These will be essential, and discussions will have to include healthcare purchasers, who undoubtedly will wish to limit its use in some way, given its expense. Local guidelines should cover:

1   selection of patients for treatment (agreed criteria);

2   agreement on which clinicians may use botulinum toxin.

9.4 Sensory impairment and pain

9.4.1 Sensory disturbance: controlling pain after stroke

Patients who have suffered a stroke may experience pain of several types. Most of the pain is mechanical, arising from reduced mobility; some will come from pre-morbid diseases such as osteoarthritis; and a minority will be specific to stroke damage (so-called central pain). Pain is often not recognised and treated.

Guidelines

a All patients should be assessed for pain on a regular basis (**C**)

b All pain should be treated actively, in accordance with the patient's wishes (**C**)

c Chronic pain, especially central pain, may respond to tricyclic antidepressants and these should be tried sooner rather than later (**A**)

d Patients with intractable pain should be referred to someone specialising in the assessment and management of pain (**C**)

Evidence (Table 9.9 p102)

There are some meta-analyses relating to pain management in general (see Cochrane reviews), and some specifically relating to central neurogenic pain. None is specific and exclusive to stroke.

a   Consensus of working party (**IV**)

b   Consensus of working party (**IV**)

c   Leijon & Boivie 1989; Wiffen et al 1999 (**Ia**)

d   Consensus of working party (**IV**)

Local guidelines

Local guidelines need to:

1   emphasise the importance of identifying and treating pain;

2   give details about local specialists in pain relief.

9.4.2 Shoulder pain

Pain in the shoulder of the affected arm is not uncommon, arising in at least 30% of all patients after stroke. It is associated with severity of disability, and is thus more common in patients in rehabilitation settings. It is not related to subluxation of the shoulder. Its relationship to handling and positioning is unstudied.

Guidelines

a The following interventions to **prevent** shoulder pain should be considered:

 i Avoiding the use of overhead arm slings, which encourage uncontrolled abduction; (**A**)

 ii Use of foam supports (**A**)

 iii Use of shoulder strapping (**B**)

 iv Education of staff and carers about correct handling of the hemiplegic arm (**B**)

b For established shoulder pain, **treatment** should:

 i start with simple interventions eg non-steroidal anti-inflammatory analgesia (**C**)

   If this does not work, treatment should include:

 ii high-intensity transcutaneous electrical nerve stimulation (**A**)

 iii three intra-articular injections of 40 mg triamcinolone (**B**)

Evidence (Table 9.10 p103)

Most studies focus on subluxation of the shoulder, but this has been shown not to be a factor in shoulder pain. Shoulder pain after stroke is strongly associated with prolonged hospital stay and poor recovery of arm function. Incorrect handling is a contributing factor in development and/or exacerbation of shoulder pain. This relationship requires further study.

a i Kumar et al 1990. A small study, and only studying one movement (**Ib**)

   ii Kotzki et al 1991. A small study only (**Ib**)

   iii Ancliffe 1992. A very small study, but with big differences shown (**IIa**)

   iv Braus et al 1994; Wanklyn et al 1996 (**III**)

b i Consensus of working party (**IV**)

   ii Leandri et al 1990. A larger study with reasonable effects shown (**Ib**)

   iii Dekker et al 1997. A small study (**IIa**)

Local guidelines

Local clinicians may wish to:

1 develop guidelines for ward staff on care of the shoulder;

2 agree how to manage pain once present.

Carer's view: She was paralysed down the right side. But because she had part use of her left hand, the nursing staff said: 'Oh, you're alright, just drag yourself up with your left hand'. Well now, any therapist would tell you that is the worst thing that you can do.

9.4.3 Sensory stimulation: acupuncture and transcutaneous electrical nerve stimulation

Transcutaneous electrical nerve stimulation (TENS) and acupuncture are both possible ways of giving sensory input, and are placed together for that reason. Their use is still being investigated; the mechanisms underlying benefit (if any) are unknown.

Guidelines

a Acupuncture should only be used in the context of ongoing trials (**A**)

b Routine TENS for improving muscle control should only be used in the context of ongoing trials (**A**)

Evidence (Table 9.11 p104)

The evidence is relatively limited, and may be subject to publication bias.

a Kjendahl et al 1997; Gosman-Hedstrom et al 1998. There are at least two well designed RCTs of reasonable size showing functional benefits, and one larger one failing to show benefit (**Ib**)

b Tekeoolu et al 1998. There is one trial showing general functional benefit, and one showing reduced motor impairment, but it is difficult to generalise from these. However, it may have a role in specific circumstances (**Ib**)

Local guidelines

These will need to detail:

1 whether acupuncture is available, the precautions needed, selection of patients;

2 how TENS machines are accessed, and selection of patients.

9.5 Drugs reducing impairment

There are many drugs that may help without directly affecting the underlying pathology. Some have already been considered (analgesia, antispastic agents etc), but there are some that do not easily fit into groups mentioned. Drugs studied include amphetamine, fluoxetine, bromocriptine, piracetam and meprobamate.

Guideline

a With the exception of analgesia, no drugs for reducing impairment should be prescribed routinely, except within the context of randomised trials (**A**)

Evidence (Table 9.12 pp104–5)

Table 9.12 shows the main randomised studies of note. Only fluoxetine and amphetamine seem consistently to be associated with benefit, but studies are too small to allow firm conclusions (**Ib**)

9.6 Functional rehabilitation interventions

See also Section 11.1

This section includes guidelines and evidence that relate to functional rehabilitation. It also includes evidence relating to equipment, on the grounds that this is part of the patient's environment and hence relevant at this level. The topics covered start with relatively restricted areas of disability (eg walking) and end considering the environment.

Patient's view: … if I'd known what I know now about strokes my life would have been easier, because eventually the Stroke Association gave me a number of books to read, so I know quite a bit about strokes. But when I wanted to know about them I didn't know.

9.6.1 Gait re-education

Recovery of independent mobility is an important goal for the immobile patient, and much therapy is devoted to gait re-education. Several of the topics considered earlier bear directly on mobility (eg botulinum toxin, balance training). Moreover, some of the evidence relating to late rehabilitation also relates to gait. This section focuses on gait re-education in the first weeks and months of rehabilitation. Treadmill training combined with the use of suspension to take some of the patient's bodyweight can be effective in regaining walking ability, when used as an adjunct to conventional therapy 3 months after acute stroke.

Guidelines

a Treadmill training with partial (<40%) bodyweight support should be considered as an adjunct to conventional therapy in patients who are not walking at 3 months after stroke (**A**)

b Gait re-education to improve walking ability should be offered, though specific techniques cannot be recommended on the basis of evidence (**B**)

Evidence (Table 9.13 pp105–6)

The evidence for treadmill training is accumulating, and this topic should be reviewed regularly. All major studies have examined treadmill training as an adjunct to conventional therapy.

a Visintin et al 1998. A reasonably large well designed study (**Ib**)

b Wall & Turnbull 1987; Richards et al 1993 (**III**)

Local guidelines

Standard treadmills are of limited value since they are unable to provide partial bodyweight support. Treadmill training has a major implication in capital cost. Local guidelines will need to consider:

1   use of treadmill with support, once available;

2   other therapeutic approaches to be used.

9.6.2 Activities of daily living

Much of stroke rehabilitation aims, directly or indirectly, to increase independence and ability in all activities of daily living (ADL), not only personal (eg dressing) but also domestic (eg cooking) and communal (eg shopping). Many of the techniques described earlier in this section might help in this task. Furthermore it has been convincingly shown that organised rehabilitation directly improves ADL. However, there is little research on direct treatment techniques.

Guidelines

a   All patients with difficulties in activities of daily living should be assessed by an occupational therapist with specialist knowledge in neurological disability (**A**)

b   Patients showing unexplained persistent difficulties in ADL should be assessed specifically for perceptual impairments (**B**)

c   Patients with difficulties in ADL should be treated by a specialist multidisciplinary team (**A**)

d   All patients must be given opportunities to practise personal ADL and, as appropriate, relevant domestic and community activities (**C**)

e   Patients should be offered advice on, and treatment aimed to achieve, employment or wanted leisure activities as appropriate (**C**)

Evidence *(Tables 3.1, 3.4, 9.3 pp79, 81, 96)*

a   Walker et al 1999 (**Ib**)

b   Lincoln et al 1997 (**IIb**)

c   Stroke Unit Trialists' Collaboration 1998 (**Ia**)

d   Consensus of working party (**IV**)

e   Consensus of working party (**IV**)

Local guidelines

These will need to specify:

1 availability of, and means of access to, therapeutic areas such as kitchens;

2 how to undertake and achieve expert advice and treatment to return to employment.

Patient's view: The problem really was in hospital ... no-one explained to me that I'd had a stroke and what's wrong with that ... small things like first when I went out to the toilet ... having a wash, but no-one explained to me, at all, that this would be a problem...No-one really explained to me 'You're not very bright on this, sort of thing, or, you know, you can't read, you can't do this, that and the other' and no-one said a damn thing to me... in hospital and I think that is wrong

Patient's admission about doing his own therapy unsupervised and without equipment: I try not to use a stick, but I paid for it because I have had two falls because I hadn't the stick with me. But I still try not to use it.

9.6.3 *Equipment and adaptations (personal aids)*

Small changes in an individual's local 'environment' can greatly increase independence: use of a wheelchair or walking stick; use of Velcro in place of buttons; use of adapted cutlery etc. Many of these 'treatments' are so simple and small that it is unlikely that anyone will ever research into them. Nonetheless there are areas of controversy such as the use of walking aids and ankle-foot orthoses. It is acknowledged that walking aids and ankle foot orthoses may benefit selected patients. This section covers small items for personal use.

Guidelines

a The need for special equipment should be assessed on an individual basis; once provided, equipment should be evaluated on a regular basis (**B**)

b Patients should be supplied as soon as possible with all aids and equipment needed (**A**)

c All patients should have easy quick access to any equipment that might increase their independence (**C**)

d Decisions must take into account the patient's (and, if necessary, the family's) views and expectations (**C**)

e Ankle-foot orthoses are of benefit for some patients (**B**)

f If an ankle-foot orthosis is supplied, it should be individually fitted (**C**)

g A walking stick may increase standing stability in patients with severe disability (**B**)

Evidence (Tables 9.14, 9.15, 9.16 pp106–8)

a   Gladman et al 1995; Mann et al 1995 (**IIa**)

b   Mann et al 1999 demonstrated cost effectiveness of equipment provision for elderly patients (not just stroke) (**Ib**)

c   Consensus of working party (**IV**)

d   Consensus of working party (**IV**)

e   Corcoran et al 1970. The evidence for ankle-foot orthoses is inconsistent; see Beckerman et al 1996a,b (**IIa**)

f   Consensus of working party (**IV**)

g   Tyson & Ashburn 1994; Lu et al 1997; Tyson et al 1998. There are only a small number of studies in this area, using small sample sizes. What there are show that using a walking aid does not encourage the patient to favour the lower limb that is unaffected (**III**)

Local guidelines

Local clinicians will need to:

1   formulate local policies concerning assessment for equipment, and its supply and retrieval;

2   agree funding arrangements and budgets with all funding organisations (eg social services);

3   ensure that orthoses are made or fitted correctly for the individual patient.

9.6.4 Equipment and adaptations (appliances)

Equipment and adaptations in this context refers to any larger items or structural changes needed to alleviate the impact of a stroke-related impairment. Many patients have residual disability that can be helped by adapting their environment on a larger scale, for example with stairlifts, hoists, perching stools or adaptations to buildings. Some of this equipment is supplied and funded by health services, a majority is supplied and funded by social services, some is funded by housing services, and some is not funded except by the patient and the family. Consequently there are major potential and actual problems in ensuring that the needs of patients are identified and then satisfied efficiently.

Guidelines

a   Every patient who is at home or leaving hospital should be assessed fully to determine whether equipment or adaptations can increase safety or independence (**A**)

b   Prescription of equipment and adaptations should be based on careful assessment of the patient and the physical and social environment in which it is to be used (**B**) c   All equipment supplied should have proven reliability and safety (**C**)

d   The patient and/or caregiver should be thoroughly trained in the safe and effective use of any equipment supplied (**C**)

e   The suitability and use of equipment should be reviewed over time as needs will change (**B**)

f   All patients should be given a contact number for future advice or help with equipment provided (**C**)

Evidence (Tables 9.14, 9.15, 9.16 pp106–8)

The evidence is largely secondary, derived from observations in RCTs or from surveys.

a   Chamberlain et al 1981; Hesse et al 1996b; Mann et al 1999 (**Ib**)

b   Gitlin et al 1993: Neville et al 1993 (**III**)

c   Gardner et al 1993 (**IV**)

d   Consensus of working party (**IV**)

e   Bynum & Rogers 1987; Sonn et al 1996 (**III**)

f   Consensus of working party (**IV**)

Local guidelines

Local guidelines will need to specify:

1   how equipment is accessed locally;

2   local eligibility criteria for each piece of equipment;

3   how it is funded locally.

Patient's view: I couldn't get in and out [of my house]... I could hardly get up my drive... I waited one full year before I could have the rail from the front door down to the gate. It took us a year to get that, and a lot of trouble for the wife.

Carer's views: We got a lot of help when he came out, more than I would have thought, but I think we're probably quite lucky living in this area because the help is there. It just appeared, all this help, I never asked for anything.

There should be somebody who actually talks to the carer and tells them about all the different facilities, you know – everyone should have somebody assigned to them.

10 Transfer back to the community

The majority of patients will be managed in hospital initially. The time of discharge from inpatient hospital care to home (or residential or nursing home care) constitutes an important watershed. There is much anecdotal and some research-based evidence that discharge is extremely poorly managed in many cases.

10.1 Discharge planning

The process of transferring responsibility for management from a specialised inpatient service, where co-ordination is relatively easy, to an outpatient or domiciliary service, or to nursing homes and residential care homes, requires considerable planning. Although this is recognised in several Department of Health circulars, insufficient attention and resources are given to the process of discharge. Discharge planning refers to any process that formally involves the team or service in transferring responsibility from one group of people or team to another.

Guidelines

a Early hospital discharge should only be considered if there is a specialist stroke rehabilitation team in the community and if the patient is able to transfer safely from bed to chair (**A**)

b Early hospital discharge to generic (non-specialist) community services should not be undertaken (**A**)

c Carers should receive all necessary equipment and training in moving and handling, in order to position and transfer the patient safely in the home environment (**B**)

d Hospital services should have a protocol and local guidelines for discharge (**A**), to check that, before discharge occurs:

   i   Patients and families are prepared and fully involved (**C**)

   ii General practitioners and primary healthcare teams, and community social services departments, are all informed (**C**)

   iii All necessary equipment and support services are in place (**C**)

   iv Any continuing treatment required should be provided without delay by a specialist service in the community, day hospital or outpatients (**A**)

   v   Patients are given information about, and offered contact with appropriate local statutory and voluntary agencies (**C**)

Evidence (Tables 3.3, 3.4, 10.1 pp80–1, 109–10)

a Rudd et al 1997; Early Supported Discharge Trialists 1999 (**Ia**)

b Ronning & Guldvog 1998b (**Ib**)

c Hakim et al 1998 (**III**)

d Evans & Hendricks 1993; Naylor et al 1994; (**Ib**)
   1–3,5 Consensus of working party (**IV**); 4. Forster et al 1999b (**Ib**)

Local guidelines

These will be essential, and must ensure that a smooth transfer of responsibility for each and every aspect of management occurs. They will need to cover:

1 discharge protocols and documentation;

2 contacting all necessary statutory organisations: who, how and when;

3 action to take if delays occur in setting up community services;

4 mechanisms to monitor process of handover;

5 names of, and methods for contacting, all relevant local voluntary agencies.

Patient's view: And when I got home there was just nothing. I was quite desperate at the time.

Carers' views: I don't think we've had any… Is it my fault, am I supposed to go and say: 'Come and help us, we need something', or is this something that should be provided automatically?

I think this is one of the problems. There's no co-operation between the various agencies, so you stand the chance of coming out and having nothing. No-one to talk to or anything.

Our doctors, district nurse and care assistants checked up on us and they came to see us when Joyce came out of hospital first, and the occupational therapy department....visited us two or three times – they lent us a ramp to get the wheelchair in and out of the house, and the wheelchair and a bath lift, which is very, very useful… then the Speech Therapy Department, I think, [referred] us to the [Stroke Association speech therapy service].

---

11 Long-term patient management

This Section covers matters that relate to the long term, after the period of 'active rehabilitation'. In most patients this phase starts soon after discharge from hospital, though for some it will not start until a programme of outpatient or domiciliary rehabilitation has been completed. This usually refers to any time after 3–6 months post-stroke.

The areas covered in this section include:

▶ episodes of further rehabilitation after discharge (11.1)

▶ post discharge social function (11.2)

▶ Secondary prevention (11.3)

Patient's view: They learned me a lot, they learned me to talk. But I couldn't walk, I came home in a wheelchair. They said you will never walk again. I thought I will. Within a month I was on a stick walking... since then – that has been five years next month. And I have persevered and I am walking and talk, thank God.

11.1 Further rehabilitation after discharge

Many patients request continuing involvement of disability services after discharge from formal rehabilitation. Usually this is rejected on the grounds that no further benefit can accrue. However, there is now evidence that, after stroke, patients show a continuing decline which can be reversed by further input.

Guidelines

a   Any patient with disability at 6 months or later after stroke should be assessed for a period of further targeted rehabilitation to be given where appropriate (**A**)

Evidence (Table 11.1 p110)

The evidence is strong and comes from controlled clinical trials investigating change in 'stable' patients, and in RCTs that focus on particular outcomes.

a   Wade et al 1992; Drummond & Walker 1995; Walker et al 1996; Werner & Kessler 1996 (**Ib**)

Local guidelines

These will need to specify:

1 mechanisms for monitoring and re-referral to specialist service(s);

2 criteria for acceptance if demand is high;

3 responsibility (health or social services) for treatments and other interventions to maintain function;

4 mechanisms to co-ordinate health and social services provision.

Carer's view: We need some help for my husband as well. If he could get more therapy. His leg is getting weaker and he can't go upstairs. So if it is getting worse and worse... after two years.,.. what's the use of that?

11.2 Post-discharge social function

After discharge the patient and family lose the social, emotional and practical support offered by an inpatient service, so support may need to be offered specifically as an additional resource.

Carer's view: You'd phone the doctor, and any time you needed he came immediately. As I say, my husband was pretty ill. He still is. If there's a problem I can phone up and I can tell him and he'll come. You know, he's very good. I just feel it's good to be able to talk to him and with all the problems ... he gives the time to listen... He gives me good support.

Guidelines

a Patients and their carers should have their individual psychosocial and support needs reviewed on a regular basis (C)

b Health and social services professionals should ensure that patients and their families have information about the statutory and voluntary organisations offering services specific to these needs (C)

c Patients who used to drive before their stroke must be given accurate up-to-date advice on their responsibilities (C)

d Patients who wish to drive should be assessed for any absolute contraindications, then for their cognitive ability to drive safely, their motor ability to control a car, and their need for any adaptations (C)

Evidence *(Table 11.2 p111)*

Whilst the only benefit shown was for improved patient and carer satisfaction where support services are provided, the consensus of working party opinion is that the correct strategies are yet to be found.

a Anderson 1992 and Pound et al 1998 show the long-term needs of patients and their carers. Evans et al 1988 showed benefits of counselling and education on problem solving and adjustment (**IV**)

b The College of Health Report showed these services provide a valuable source of comfort (Kelson) 1998 (**IV**)

c Driver and Vehicle Licensing Authority (DVLA) booklet (**IV**)

d Extrapolation from Nouri & Lincoln 1993 (**IV**)

Local guidelines

Local health and social commissioners will have to agree:

1 policies on providing financial support to voluntary organisations giving longer-term support to disabled patients;

2 how services are accessed, and by whom.

Stroke services will need to:

1 obtain and use a DVLA advice booklet (address in Appendix 3)

2 agree protocols on assessing patients for driving safety;

3 collate and provide information on local resources able to assess driving and advise on adaptations.

Patient's view of Stroke Association stroke clubs: The best time I had after my stroke really is the stroke club that I went to… and I am very glad [to have the opportunity] really to thank them specially… the most support I got is from the stroke club.

Patient's view on Stroke Association volunteers visiting them at home: They do a marvellous job… people from Stroke, yes they come to my house to see me… marvellous they come.

Carer's view of Different Strokes: The main thing is that Different Strokes is so much more personal and also that it caters for younger stroke survivors.

Carer's view of Different Strokes' exercise meetings: He loves it, he comes alive… They're all the same and they know what each other has gone through. He enjoys the exercise and they're such a friendly bunch. There's no pressure. It's wonderful. We come every week.

Carer's views: In the ... borough still there is a respite care package. You say, look I need a week away from it all –[he] either goes into respite care and lives there residential for a week or a fortnight or a month or whatever. But that is done through social services. And you have to press them a bit you know.

[You need] a sort of a named person... who can link all the different agencies... [and] somebody you can contact if you need help.

11.3 Secondary prevention

Patients who have suffered a stroke remain at an increased risk of a further stroke (about 7% per annum), of other vascular events (about 7% per annum) and of epilepsy (about 5% in 2 years). The risk of further stroke is highest early after stroke. Therefore there should be a high priority given to secondary prevention.

Guidelines

These guidelines apply to **all patients**, even those not admitted to hospital. Therefore they refer to patients either **before discharge from hospital** or **before 4 weeks have passed from stroke onset**, whichever is the sooner.

a   All patients should have their blood pressure checked, and hypertension persisting for over one month should be treated. The British Hypertension Society guidelines are: Optimal blood pressure treatment targets are systolic blood pressure <140 mmHg and diastolic blood pressure <85 mmHg; the minimum accepted level of control recommended is <150/ <90 mmHg (**A**)

b   All patients, not on anticoagulation, should be taking aspirin (50–300 mg) daily (**A**), or a combination of low-dose aspirin and dipyridamole modified release (MR). Where patients are aspirin intolerant an alternative antiplatelet agent (clopidogrel 75mg daily or dipyridamole MR 200mg twice daily) should be used (**A**)

c   Anticoagulation should be started in every patient in atrial fibrillation (valvular or non-valvular) unless contraindicated (**A**)

d   Anticoagulation should be considered for all patients who have ischaemic stroke associated with mitral valve disease, prosthetic heart valves, or within 3 months of myocardial infarction (**C**)

e   Anticoagulation should not be started until brain imaging has excluded haemorrhage, and 14 days have passed from the onset of an ischaemic stroke (**A**)

f   Anticoagulation should not be used after transient ischaemic attacks or minor strokes unless cardiac embolism is suspected (**A**)

g   Any patient with a carotid artery area stroke, and minor or absent residual disability should be considered for carotid endarterectomy (**A**)

h   Carotid ultrasound should be performed on all patients who would be considered for carotid endarterectomy (**C**)

i   Carotid endarterectomy should only be undertaken by a specialist surgeon with a proven low complication rate, and only if the stenosis is measured at greater than 70% (**A**)

j   All patients should be assessed for other vascular risk factors and be treated or advised appropriately (**B**)

k   All patients should be given appropriate advice on lifestyle factors (such as not smoking, regular exercise, diet, achieving a satisfactory weight, reducing the use of added salt) (**C**)

l   Therapy with a statin should be considered for all patients with a past history of myocardial infarction and a cholesterol >5.0 mmol/l following stroke (**A**)

Evidence (Tables 11.3, 11.4 p111–4)

Much of the evidence is derived from research into primary prevention, but there are now also studies investigating secondary prevention.

a   Post Stroke Antihypertensive Treatment Study collaborative group 1995; Ramsay et al 1999 (British Hypertension Society guidelines) (**Ib**)

b   Antiplatelet Trialists Collaboration 1994 (**Ia**); CAPRIE 1996; Diener et al 1996 (**Ib**)

c   European Atrial Fibrillation Trial (EAFT) study group, 1993, 1995 (**Ia**)

d   Consensus of working party (**IV**)

e   European Atrial Fibrillation Trial 1993, 1995, and consensus of working party (**Ib**)

f   Stroke Prevention in Reversible Ischaemia Trial 1997 (**Ib**)

g   European Carotid Surgery Trialists' Collaborative Group 1998; North American Symptomatic Carotid Endarterectomy Trial Collaborators 1998 (**Ib**)

h   Consensus of working party (**IV**)

i   Cina et al 1999 (**Ib**)

j   Hebert et al 1997 (**IIa**)

k   Consensus of working party; Elliott et al 1996; Midgley et al 1996; Cutler et al 1997; Whelton et al 1998 (**IV**)

l   Blauw et al 1997; Hebert et al 1997; Crouse et al 1997, 1998. The evidence for patients with previous myocardial infarction shows reduction in stroke incidence. The mean age of patients in the trials was <60 years, predominantly male, with low incidence of hypertension (**Ia**)

Local guidelines

These will be need to specify local policies for:

1 antiplatelet treatments, taking into consideration the cost implications of implementing routine use of agents other than aspirin;

2 referral to specialist vascular surgeons for carotid surgery;

3 controlling anticoagulation;

4 cholesterol lowering drugs;

5 dietary advice and follow-up.

Service evaluation

12 Service evaluation

This Section discusses various ways in which quality might be improved, and the data that might be used in order to achieve this. Matters that may need to be considered include: sources of data, especially routine hospital data; documentation; outcome assessment; adjusting for case-mix; measuring structure and process.

Service evaluation needs to cover not only individual professions and departments but also the quality of the whole service, including care in the community.

12.1 Data collection

See also Section 4.1

In order to provide and monitor an adequate clinical service, information is required. Clinical audit depends upon identifying cases and retrieving information from patient records. The standard of note keeping varies widely, and the means of recording information is even more varied. Most commonly each profession keeps its own set of notes, and there is minimal sharing of information. Consequently the ability to abstract standard data for audit purposes, as well as communication between professionals, is severely impeded. Outcomes are rarely if ever recorded routinely on all patients in a standard way. The Intercollegiate Working Party for Stroke has produced both multidisciplinary and profession-specific stroke audit proformas, obtainable from the publications department at the Royal College of Physicians.

Guidelines

a Clinicians should take responsibility for all aspects of data collection:

  i keeping a stroke register (**B**), because routine hospital statistics do not accurately count stroke patients;

  ii providing leadership in clinical audit

b Service providers should consider using a specific, structured set of documentation to follow the patient throughout his/her illness (**B**)

c All parties involved in assessing outcome should agree on the areas of outcome to be measured (**C**)

d Once agreed, suitable measures should be chosen, taking into account validity, reliability, relevance, simplicity and resource implications (**C**)

Evidence *(Tables 12.1, 12.2 pp114–7)*

a   Mant et al 1997 (**IIa**)

b   Stineman & Granger 1998 (**IIa**)

c   Consensus of working party (**IV**)

d   Duncan et al 1995 (**IV**)

Local guidelines

Local services will need to:

1   agree the classification of stroke that is to be used;

2   discuss areas likely to benefit from standard documentation;

3   agree on areas of important outcome applicable to all patients, and how they are to be measured.

12.2   Data interpretation

Any observed outcome cannot be attributed solely to the structure and process of the service. Contextual factors (cf WHO ICIDH, Table 2.1), specifically the characteristics of the patient and environmental characteristics, will have a greater or lesser impact upon the final outcome. Further, the outcome will be affected by the nature and severity of the stroke itself.

Guidelines

a   Data analysis, and especially comparative or evaluative analysis should only be undertaken cautiously (**B**)

b   Assessing the quality and effectiveness of services should concentrate upon recording process measures, rather than outcome, until improvements are made in methods of risk adjustment for case-mix (**B**)

Evidence *(Tables 12.2, 12.3 pp116–8)*

a   Poloniecki, 1998; Poloniecki et al, 1998 (**IIa**)

b   Jessee & Schranz 1990; Shah et al 1990; Mant & Hicks 1995 (**IIa**)

Local guidelines

Local guidelines will need to:

1   consider using a standardised audit package, eg the Royal College of Physicians Stroke Audit;

2   discuss how outcome data collected routinely are to be used to improve quality without over-interpretation of data and differences;

3   consider what aspect of the process is indicative of quality and what is amenable to data collection on a systematic or random basis.

12.3   Patient and carer opinions

The perceptions of service users are an important way of evaluating service delivery, as demonstrated in the report by the College of Health on the views of patients and their carers for the development of these guidelines.

Guidelines

a   Districts should consider ways in which the views of patients and carers can be incorporated into service evaluations (**B**)

b   Plans for service developments should include the opinions of patients and carers, either through local organisations who can represent them, or through specifically organised local groups of patients and carers (**C**)

Evidence (Table 12.2 pp116–7)

a   Consensus of working party; and extrapolation from Scholte op Reimer et al 1996; Pound et al 1999 (**III**)

b   Consensus of working party (**IV**)

Tables of evidence

These tables list most of the evidence collected and collated to inform the guidelines. In each table there is a consistent order: the first section includes systematic reviews and metal-analyses, and the second section includes trials and observational studies. Within each section the references are in date order. Each table gives a reference, a brief description of the sample studies and the design, a brief description of the subject of the study (eg the intervention), and a brief conclusion or comment. Readers are recommended to read the original references if they want more detail.

Table 3.1 Organisation of stroke care: specialised services

Source	Design and sample	Intervention(s)	Conclusions
Stroke Unit Trialists' Collaboration, 1998	M/A; n = 19 RCTs, n = 2060 patients	Stroke unit care or general medical ward care	Stroke unit care reduces mortality and morbidity with no increase in length of stay
Dekker et al, 1998	S/R; n = 7 trials, n = 1133 patients	Day hospital outpatient rehabilitation or routine care/domiciliary care/nil	No firm conclusions can be drawn
Kalra, 1994	RCT; n = 141; middle-band stroke patients	Stroke unit or general medical ward	Stroke unit patients recovered faster, and more, and had shorter length of stay despite less total therapy time
Laursen et al, 1995	RCT; n = 65 acute stroke patients	Stroke unit or general ward	Stroke unit discharged fewer to nursing home
Logan et al, 1997	RCT; n = 111; stroke patients after discharge	Enhanced domiciliary OT: or normal social services OT service	Enhanced service reduced carer distress, and improved patient function
Indredavik et al, 1997	RCT; n = 220; 5 year follow-up on acute patients	Specialist stroke unit or general medical ward	Stroke unit benefits sustained; less disability, more at home, fewer deaths
Ronning & Guldvog, 1998a	RCT*; n = 550; acute stroke patients admitted	Specialist stroke ward or general medical ward; both short-stay (<14 days)	Specialist ward was more likely to intervene medically, and reduced stroke stroke recurrence
Indredavik et al, 1998	RCT; n = 87; 5 year follow-up on acute patients	Speciallist stroke unit or general medical ward	Stroke unit associated with more social activities and less emotional distress

MA   Meta-analysis
OT   Occupational Therapy
RCT   Randomised Controlled Trial (* = quasi-random by date of birth)
S/R   Systematic Review

Table 3.2 Training of staff

Source	Design & Sample	Intervention(s)	Conclusions
Jones et al, 1998	RCT; n = 6 wards, 59 nurses, 38 stroke patients; 1000 obs	Two two-hour lectures on stroke and rehabilitation	Teaching increased knowledge and changed practice, but effects small
Forster et al, 1999a	CCT; n = 32 nurses, two stroke wards	Training programme: three two-hour sessions	Improved transfer technique, altered attitudes; but many areas still 'poor'

CCT   Controlled clinical trial
RCT   Randomised controlled trial

Table 3.3 Organisation of care: early discharge to community services

Source	Design & Sample	Intervention(s)	Conclusions
Shepperd & Iliffe, 1997	*M/A; n = 5 trials, 747 patients; very different groups, none stroke*	*Hospital-at-home or inpatient hospital care*	*Insufficient evidence to warrant change of practice*
Early Supported Discharge Trialists, 1999	M/A: 4 trials; n = selected group of elderly stroke patients	Early discharge with community based rehabilitation from specialist team	Early supported discharge can reduce length of stay for selected patients. The relative risks and benefits and overall costs remain unclear
Rudd et al, 1997	RCT; n = 331; patients able to transfer	Specialist community team made available, compared with routine service	Disabled patients discharged 6 days earlier; no detriment and possible increase in satisfaction with hospital care
Rodgers et al, 1997	RCT; n = 92; discharged patients after acute stroke	Early supported discharge to specialist team, or routine services	Early discharge feasible, saving 9 days as inpatient, and no obvious detriment
Holmqvist et al, 1998	RCT; n = 81; acute stroke, in hospital >5 days	Specialist, multidisciplinary outreach rehabilitation service, or routine care	Patients discharged 15 days earlier; disability levels the same, possibly more distress
Ronning & Guldvog, 1998b *	RCT; n = 251; patients 7–14 days post-stroke	Organised specialist inpatient rehabilitation or community rehabilitation	Non-specialist, un-co-ordinated community rehabilitation associated with more mortality and morbidity
Shepperd et al, 1998a,b	*RCT; n = 538 patients; need acute admission,* **or** *already in hospital*	*Hospital-at-home or inpatient hospital care*	*No differences in outcomes; no cost difference, but costs shifted to primary care*
Richards et al, 1998 Coast et al, 1998	*RCT; n = 241 patients, all in hospital*	*Hospital-at-home or inpatient hospital care*	*No differences in outcomes; hospital-at-home cheaper*
Beech et al, 1999 Rudd et al, 1997	RCT; n = 331 acute stroke patients; economic evaluation	Early supported discharge vs conventional care	Early discharge is unlikely to lead to financial savings. Its main benefit is to release capacity for expanding in-patient stroke caseload.

M/A   Meta-analysis
RCT   Randomised controlled trial (* = quasi-random by date of birth)
Entries in italic denote studies that are not specific to stroke.

Table 3.4 Use of day hospitals/domiciliary rehabilitation

Source	Design & Sample	Intervention(s)	Conclusions
Dekker et al, 1998	S/R; n = 6 trials (all included below)	Day hospital #(DH)# rehabilitation for stroke	No conclusions as (a) no definition of DH, (b) varied outcome measures, (c) varied control groups
Forster et al, 1999b	S/R; 12 trials; n = 2867	Day hospital vs comprehensive care (5 trials); domiciliary care (4 trials); no comprehensive care (3 trials)	Day hospital may be effective for elderly people needing rehabilitation, but has no clear advantage over other comprehensive care.
Smith et al, 1981a	RCT; n = 133 patients discharged disabled, and fit enough to attend 5 x/week	Three intensities hospital outpatient therapy: 5 days/week; 3 days/week; zero	Positive dose-response relationship found; hospital outpatient specialist rehabilitation helped and sustained
Tucker et al, 1984	*RCT; n = 120 patients needing rehabilitation (65 with stroke)*	*Day hospital 2–3 days/week, 5 hours/day; 6–8 weeks or normal services*	*Unsustained increase in independence, sustained mood improvement; cost 30% more*
Cummings et al, 1985	*RCT; n = 96 disabled people, mixed aetiology including stroke*	*Five days/week or intensive inpatient rehabilitation*	*No difference in disability outcome; day hospital more cost-effective with given costing assumptions*
Eagle et al, 1991	*RCT; 113 patients with disability needing rehabilitation*	*Day hospital or conventional geriatric outpatient service*	*No difference in outcome*
Young & Forster, 1992, 1993	RCT; n = 124 patients discharged with disability	Specialist domiciliary therapy or specialist DH rehabilitation	Disability lessened more with home physiotherapy, which was also cheaper
Gladman et al, 1993, 1994 Gladman & Lincoln, 1994	RCT; n = 327 patients discharged with disability from 3 services: specialist elderly; general medical; or stroke unit	Specialist domiciliary rehabilitation, or routine day hospital or outpatient services	No overall difference in outcome (may be subgroup differences, but disappeared by 12 months); cost differences varied between groups
Hui et al, 1995	RCT; n = 120; elderly acute stroke patients	Neurology team (no day hospital) or geriatric team with day hospital	Care in the geriatric day hospital hastened functional recovery at no greater cost
Corr & Bayer, 1995	RCT; n = 110 stroke patients at discharge from stroke unit	Occupational therapist (OT) visits at home, or routine services	OT visits increased use of aids and reduced readmission rate
Duncan et al 1998	RCT; n = 42 minimally and moderately impaired stroke patients 30–90 days after stroke	Therapist supervised exercises 3 times per week for 8 weeks versus usual care after discharge	Continuing therapy exercises after discharge probably improves mobility.
Walker et al, 1999	RCT; n = 185; stroke patients 1 month after stroke	5 months of occupational therapy at home vs no intervention	Occupational Therapy significantly reduced disability and handicap in patients with stroke who were not admitted to hospital

RCT   Randomised controlled trial
S/R   Systematic review (not a meta-analysis)
Entries in italic denote studies that are not specific to stroke.

Table 3.5 Organisation: other relevant studies

Source	Design & Sample	Intervention(s)	Conclusions
Landefeld et al, 1995	*RCT; n = 651 acutely ill hospital admissions aged 70+*	*Routine care, or special unit with (a) good environment, (b) patient-centred care with protocols, (c) discharge planning, (d) specialist medical input*	*Specialised unit reduced dependence and discharge to nursing home*
Webb et al, 1995	CCT; 6 years of practice; in 3 services	Implementation of stroke team for one service	Reduced length of stay in service with team after its introduction
Gompertz et al, 1995	CCT; n = 261 acute strokes; two adjacent health districts	One had comprehensive stroke service with stroke unit, the other did not. But many other differences between districts	No observed difference in process or outcome; effect of stroke service will depend upon context

CCT Controlled Clinical Trial
RCT Randomised Controlled Trial
Entries in italic denote studies that are not specific to stroke.

Table 3.6 Acute home care

Source	Design & Sample	Intervention(s)	Conclusions
Langhorne et al, 1999	M/A; 4 trials; n = 921 stroke patients	'Hospital at home' for acute stroke	Trend toward greater hospital bed use and increased costs in 'hospital at home' intervention group
Wade et al, 1985a,b	CCT; n = 857 acute stroke (first & recurrent)	Additional team available to patients at home	No effect on admission rate or length of stay, or disability outcome
Shepperd et al, 1998a,b	*RCT; n = 538 patients (few with stroke); need acute admission, **or** already in hospital*	*Hospital-at-home or inpatient hospital care*	*No differences in outcomes; no cost difference, but costs shifted to primary care*

CCT Controlled clinical trial
M/A Meta-analysis
RCT Randomised controlled trial
Entries in italic denote studies that are not specific to stroke.

Table 3.7 Use of protocols
(Note: Studies not specific to stroke)

Source	Design & Sample	Intervention(s)	Conclusions
Naylor, 1990	RCT; n = 40 hospitalised elderly	Comprehensive discharge planning protocol for elderly	Fewer readmissions
Lilford et al, 1992	RCT; n = 2424 first antenatal visits	Unstructured questionnaire (normal form); structured questionnaire; computer-based questionnaire	Structured questionnaire increased information obtained and increased number of effective actions
Naylor et al, 1994	RCT; n = 276 patients aged 70+ years	Comprehensive discharge planning protocol for elderly	Protocol led to shorter admission and fewer readmissions
Bowen & Yaste, 1994	CCT; n = 386 acute stroke admissions	Protocol, with critical nursing pathway (design: before/after, and with/without)	Protocol led to lower hospital costs, and possible reduction in length of stay
Duncan et al, 1995	CCT (before/after); n = 126 patients; notes review	Set-up of acute stroke unit with rehabilitation stroke unit, and protocols	Mortality reduced from 40% to 22%
Vissers et al, 1996	RCT; n = 8 doctors and 233 patients	Computer-given protocol for management of fracture, or normal management	Outcome improved by protocol **only if** correct diagnosis made initially
Vallet et al, 1997	RCT; n = 24 patients with COAD	Training programme individualised or standardised	Individualised protocol more effective
Kollef et al, 1997	RCT; n = 357 patients on mechanical ventilation	Protocol-directed or physician-directed weaning from ventilator	Protocol direction safe and more efficient (quicker by 20%), and saved $42,000

CCT Controlled clinical trial.
COAD Chronic obstructive airways disease
RCT Randomised controlled trial

Table 4.1 Assessment
(Note: Studies not specific to stroke)

Source	Design & Sample	Intervention(s)	Conclusions
Stuck et al, 1993	M/A; n = 28 trials, 9871 elderly patients	Comprehensive geriatric assessment (CGA) or routine medical care	CGA linked to co-ordinated management improved survival and function
Cunningham et al, 1996	Obs; n = 30 patients and 4 professions	Detection of disability outside own area	Low levels of agreement/detection between professions
Wikander et al, 1998	RCT; n = 34 acute stroke patients with urinary incontinence	Ward using structured assessment with FIM, or ward using Bobath clinical assessment	Structured assessment led to urinary continence being achieved more frequently

FIM Functional independence measure (an assessment of disability)
M/A Meta-analysis
Obs Observational study
RCT Randomised controlled trial

Table 4.2 Goal setting in rehabilitation
(Note: these are intervention studies, and are not specific to stroke, except for study marked *)

Source	Design & Sample	Intervention(s)	Conclusions
Greenfield et al, 1985	RCT; n = 45; patients with peptic ulcer	Routine education, or coaching with own medical records	Active, personal involvement reduced disability and handicap but not impairment
Berry et al, 1989	RCT; n = 77; enlisted military personnel	No instruction, or goal setting ± goal attainment	To achieve change must set goals and teach how to change
Kennedy et al, 1991	CCT; n = 20; patients with spinal injury	No goal planning, then goal planning	Goal planning associated with less time disengaged
Stenstrom, 1994	RCT; n = 42; patients with rheumatoid arthritis	Pain control techniques or goal setting techniques	Goal setting increased activity and decreased pain
Bar-Eli et al, 1994	RCT; n = 80; adolescents with disturbed behaviour	Long-term goals or long- and short-term goals	Adding short-term goals increased improvement in muscular performance
Webb & Glueckauf, 1994	RCT; n = 16; head injured patients	Low or high involvement in goal planning	Increased involvement led to maintenance of gains
*van Vliet et al, 1995	CCT; n = 5 patients after stroke	Goal directed or non-goal directed movement (otherwise similar)	Goal directed movement (reaching and grasping) more kinematically normal
Landefeld et al, 1995	RCT; n = 651 acutely ill hospital admissions aged 70+	Routine care, or special unit with (a) good environment (b) patient-centred care with protocols, (c) discharge planning, (d) specialist medical input	Specialised unit reduced dependence and discharge to nursing home
Blair, 1995 Blair et al, 1996	RCT; n = 79; nursing home residents	Routine care; or mutual goal setting ± behaviour modification	Combination of goal setting and behaviour modification reduced dependence in ADL
Glasgow et al, 1996, 1997	RCT; n = 206; people with diabetes	Routine care, or patient-centred goal setting (20 minutes) aided by computer assessment	Goal setting led to prolonged change in dietary behaviour
Theodorakis et al, 1997	RCT; n = 37; injured sports students	Training alone, or setting specific goals and giving feedback	Performance (strength) improved more in trial group
Johnson et al, 1997	RCT; n = 52; people with learning disability	Strategy instruction ± goal setting ± self instruction	Goal setting and self instruction did not improve reading
Bar-Eli et al, 1997	RCT; n = 346; high-school students	Strength training with differing levels of target and differing practice intensity	Moderate/hard specific goals led to more strength gain than easy or unachievable goals or non-specific goals
Vallet et al, 1997	RCT; n = 24 people with chronic airway limitation	Standard (routine) goals or individualised goals for fitness training	Individualised goals more efficient and effective

ADL   Activities of daily living
CCT   Controlled clinical trial (not randomised)
RCT   Randomised controlled trial

Table 4.3 Therapeutic approaches

Source	Design & Sample	Intervention(s)	Conclusions
Logigian et al, 1983	CCT; n = 42 acute stroke patients	Traditional therapy, or facilitatory (Bobath, Rood)	No differences found
Dickstein et al, 1986	CCT; n = 131 acute stroke patients	Functional, or PNF, or Bobath approach	No long-term differences seen (Bobath slower at regaining gait independence)
Lord & Hall, 1986	CCT; n = 39 patients in two centres	One centre was traditional, the other neuromuscular training techniques	No difference seen
Basmajian et al, 1987	RCT; n = 29 stroke patients	Bobath approach or behavioural approach to arm therapy	Outcome the same; no differences seen
Jongbloed et al, 1989	RCT; n = 90; stroke within 12 weeks	Functional approach, or sensorimotor integrative approach to occupational therapy (Bobath/Rood)	No difference in outcome
Wagenaar et al, 1990	CCT; n = 7 acute stroke patients	Bobath and Brunnestrom approaches compared	No significant or systematic difference in effects
Nelson et al, 1996	RCT; n = 26 post-stroke patients	Functional task (game, tipping dice) or exercise (identical rotation movement)	Functional task greatly increased supination of forearm
Dean & Shepherd, 1997	RCT; n = 20; stroke 1+ years ago	Training at reaching (functional), against cognitive training	Task-related training improved ability at similar tasks
Patel et al, 1998	CCT; n = 184; acute stroke	Unit with impairment-focused approach, and unit with functionally oriented approach	Similar disability and placement outcomes; length of stay 25% shorter in functionally oriented unit

CCT   Controlled clinical trial
PNF   Proprioceptive neuromuscular facilitation
RCT   Randomised controlled trial

Table 4.4 Intensity of therapy input

Source	Design & Sample	Intervention(s)	Conclusions
Richards et al, 1993 (see also Malouin et al, 1992)	RCT; n = 27 acute stroke patients	Early, intense conventional therapy; later less intense conventional therapy; early intense gait and muscle retraining	Early muscle retraining and gait retraining (on treadmill) facilitated gait recovery; no differences between conventional groups
Langhorne et al, 1996	M/A; n = 7 trials, 597 stroke patients	Physiotherapy after stroke	More physiotherapy input was associated with a reduction in death and deterioration
Kwakkel et al, 1997	M/A; n = 9 trials, 1051 stroke patients	Daily rate of physiotherapy or occupational therapy	Higher rate of therapy associated with better outcome; but many confounding factors
Smith et al, 1981a	RCT; n = 133 patients after discharge	Three intensities hospital outpatient therapy: 5 days/week; 3 days/week; zero	Dose-response effect seen; but many patients unable to tolerate high intensity input
Rapoport & Eerd, 1989	CCT; n = 273 (102 with acute stroke)	Physiotherapy over weekend (reorganisation of schedule, cost neutral)	Stroke patients had a shorter length of stay
Carey, 1990	RCT; n = 16; long-term arm disability after stroke	Manual stretching of finger flexor muscles for five minutes, or none	Control of finger movements improved after stretch (but spasticity unaffected)
Sunderland et al, 1992, 1994	RCT; n = 132 acute stroke patients	Routine therapy, or enhanced (more and different) therapy for arm	Faster recovery if some arm movement present initially, but no long-term difference
Feys et al, 1998	RCT; n = 100 stroke patients 3–5 weeks post-stroke	Routine therapy with additional: attention only, or sensorimotor stimulation	Additional therapy reduced motor loss (impairment) but not arm disability
Kwakkel et al, 1999	RCT; n = 101 severely disabled patients with primary middle-cerebral-artery stroke	Arm training; leg training vs control programme of arm and leg immobilised with an inflatable pressure splint for 30 minutes, 5 days a week for 20 weeks after stroke	Greater intensity of leg training improved functional recovery and status; greater intensity of arm training improved dexterity
Lincoln et al, 1999 Parry et al, 1999	RCT; 282 acute stroke patients	Routine physiotherapy for the arm vs 10 additional hours with qualified physio vs additional treatment from trained therapy assistant under supervision, for 5 weeks after stroke	Patients with severe arm impairment did not improve in any group. In less severe patients significant benefits were found in those who completed the treatment (repetitive supervised practice of movements) with the trained assistant

CCT   Controlled clinical trial
M/A   Meta-analysis
RCT   Randomised controlled trial

Table 5.1 Stress on carers

Source	Design & Sample	Intervention(s)	Conclusions
Anderson, 1992	Obs; n = 173 stroke patients (aged 60 or over) and their family carers	Interviews of patients and carers at 4 weeks, 9 and 18 months after stroke	Demonstrated experience of stroke illness (physical, social, economic and emotional effects) + patterns of coping
Flaherty et al, 1992	*Obs; 148 carers of chronically disabled older people*	*Relationship of stress to urinary incontinence*	*Stress related to patient's urinary incontinence and cognitive loss*
Draper et al, 1992	Obs; 99 carers of patients with stroke or dementia	Relationship of stress to patient characteristics, including diagnosis	Stressors similar in both diagnoses: patient's behaviour and mood both important stressors
Williams, 1994	Obs; 29 carers of stroke patients	Questionnaires on stressors investigating behaviours and effect of behaviours	Commonest stressors were patient irritability, dependence, and immature behaviour
Anderson et al, 1995	Obs; 84 carers of disabled stroke survivors	Relationship of carer stress to patient dependence and other factors	Half showed emotional stress, related mostly to cognitive losses or behavioural problems in patients
Fredman & Daly, 1997	Obs; 200 carers (64 patients had stroke)	Self-reported weight change related to other measures of stress	Self-reported weight loss of 10+ pounds associated with stress
Pound et al, 1998	Obs; n = 40 patients selected from a hospital stroke register	Interview 10 months post-stroke	Showed physical and social difficulties post-stroke.
Scholte op Reimer et al, 1998a	Obs; n = 166 and 47; carers 6 months and 17 months post-stroke	Study of validity and reliability of Sense of competence questionnaire (SCQ)	SCQ (27 questions) can assess burden of care-giving
Dennis et al, 1998	Obs; n = 246 carers at 6 months post-stroke	Frequency of distress, and factors associated with carer distress	About half of carers distressed. Related to patient's ADL dependence, mood state, and pre-stroke dependence
Scholte op Reimer et al, 1998b	Obs; n = 115 carers at 3 years post-stroke	Multivariate analysis of factors associated with burden of care	Main factors were: carers' emotional distress; patient dependence/disability; loneliness; carers' disability and unmet needs for support

ADL   Activities of Daily Living
Obs   Observational study
Entry in italic denote studies that are not specific to stroke

Table 5.2 Studies on information giving

Source	Design & Sample	Intervention(s)	Conclusions
Lomer & McLellan 1987	RCT; n = 48 patients and 44 relatives after admission for stroke	Information leaflet on stroke	Showed increased knowledge about stroke illness, treatment and prognosis. No effect on knowledge of services
Pain & McLellan, 1990	RCT; n = 36 stroke patients discharged	Sending of personalised information booklet	No difference in social or physical activities; information and stress not assessed
Bertakis, 1991	*RCT; n = 214 new patients in family practice*	*Booklet with or without educational presentation on use of booklet*	*Total use of health services unchanged; but judged to make more appropriate use of services*
O'Mahony et al, 1997	Obs; n = 76 community stroke patients	Assessment of satisfaction with information and advice given on extant problems	More advice and/or better means of giving advice and information needed
Clark & Smith, 1998	Obs; n = 60 stroke patients in rehabilitation unit	Multivariate analysis of factors relating to satisfaction with progress	More satisfaction with service associated with more information about stroke and services
Mant et al,1998	RCT; n = 93, acute stroke patients and their carers	Information pack for patients and carers after stroke	Showed differences in knowledge; no differences in satisfaction with or use of services; no differences in mood or quality of life (SF-36)

Obs   Observational study
RCT   Randomised controlled trial
SF-36 Shortform 36 (a measure of outcome)
Entry in italic denotes study that is not specific to stroke

Table 6.1 Diagnosis of stroke

Source	Design & Sample	Findings	Conclusions
Twomey, 1978	Obs; 1004 admissions with stroke over 7 years	30 tumours: 13 secondary tumours; 12 malignant primaries; 5 benign primaries	Tumours presenting as stroke are relatively rare, and are rarely benign
von Arbin et al, 1981	Obs; 206 referrals to stroke unit	6 not stroke: 2 myocardial infarction; and 1 each: meningitis, post-epileptic, Bell's palsy, meningioma	Diagnosis within 24 hours by two physicians (junior and senior) rarely incorrect
Norris & Hachinski, 1982	Obs; 821 referrals to stroke ward	108 not stroke: 42 post-epileptic, 9 malignant tumours, 3 subdural	Accuracy improved by experience of clinician and time, **not** by CT scan
Chambers et al, 1983	Obs; n = 700 stroke unit referrals	84 (12%) non-stroke: migraine (23), tumours (12), psychogenic (12), SAH (6) etc	All admitted with clinical diagnosis; misdiagnosis occurs but only 18/84 shown on CT scan
Sandercock et al, 1985	Obs; 736 referrals with suspected stroke	132 clinically not stroke; 5 'stroke' had tumours or subdural haemorrhage; 3 'non-stroke' had stroke	Clinical diagnosis by experienced clinician is sound

Table 6.1 continued

Source	Design & Sample	Findings	Conclusions
Sotaniemi et al, 1990	Obs; 1191 patients having CT scan (n = 254 clinically stroke)	Of 254 clinical stroke, 66 had 'other' findings, Including 4 with tumour; of 805 clinically not stroke, 30 had stroke	Suggests CT scans can discover alternative diagnoses. Unusually high 'mis-diagnosis' rate
Ricci et al, 1991	Obs; 379 clinical strokes scanned	4 non-stroke lesions on CT scan: 3 malignant tumours and 1 subdural haemorrhage	One experienced clinician can usually make diagnosis correctly
Kothari et al,1995a	Obs: 74 stroke patients, and 225 non-stroke	Use of abbreviated neurological scale for triage of stroke patients out of hospital	Three items identified 100% of stroke patients: facial palsy, motor arm and dysarthria
Kothari et al, 1995b	Obs; n = 441; diagnosis of admitting doctor compared with discharge diagnosis	Of 427 discharged, 422 correctly identified: of 441 admitted; 422 correct	Admitting doctor's diagnosis (with CT scan) usually correct (in USA)
Sagar et al, 1996	Obs; n = 435 patients with acute stroke	373 had chest x-ray: 31 clinically relevant findings, 14 changed management; 77% technically poor	Routine chest X-ray is not warranted, and is rarely of adequate quality
Martin et al, 1997	Obs; n = 508 referrals with minor stroke or TIA	Agreed TIA/stroke in 373; but vascular area in only 315. No single alternative diagnosis stands out	Patients referred for carotid surgery need careful neurological evaluation first
Ferro et al, 1998	Obs; n = 185; general practitioner and admitting doctor stroke diagnoses compared with neurologist's	44/52 GP diagnoses correct; 169/185 admitting doctor diagnoses confirmed; 3 tumours and 1 subdural	Routine clinical diagnosis is robust; absent or unusual history increases error

GP   General practitioner (Family Doctor)
Obs   Observational study
SAH   Subarachnoid haemorrhage
TIA   Transient ischaemic attack
CT   Computerised tomography

Table 6.2 Diagnosis of transient ischaemic attacks

Source	Design & Sample	Findings	Conclusions
Levy, 1988	Obs; 80 members of neurology department; median (IQR) age 36 (31–42)	25 (32%; 95% CI 21–44%) had transient neurological episodes with no pathology	Transient symptoms like TIAs are common in healthy young people
Bots et al, 1997	Obs; 7983 people aged 55+; Rotterdam	239 had transient neurological attacks in last 3 years; only 118 were TIAs; both increased with age	Prevalence of TIAs with 3 years was 1.6/1000 aged 55+; half of all transient neurological attacks are not TIAs
Lemesle et al, 1998	Obs; 283 clinical TIAs on population-based register	25 not TIA: subdural haematoma 12, tumour 8, haemorrhage 5	Transient neurological symptoms need careful diagnosis

CI   Confidence intervals
IQR   Interquartile range
Obs   Observational study
TIA   Transient ischaemic attack

Table 7.1 Specific treatment (drugs and surgery) of acute stroke: *Cochrane reviews*
(Date indicates when last substantive update was made to the review)

Source	Design & Sample	Intervention(s)	Conclusions
a'Rogvi-Hansen & Boysen, 1994	M/A; n = 6 trials, 554 patients	Intravenous **glycerol** within first four days	Possible short-term reduction in mortality, but data insufficient to be certain
Bath et al, 1996	M/A; n = 5 trials, 793 patients	**Methylxanthines** (e.g. pentoxifylline) within one week	Insufficient data to draw conclusions
Bath & Bath, 1996	M/A; n = 5 trials, 191 patients	**Prostacyclin** or analogue within 7 days of stroke	Insufficient data to draw any conclusions
Liu & Wardlaw, 1996	M/A; n = 3 trials, 182 patients	**Fibrinogen depleting** agents started within 14 days of acute stroke	Insufficient data to draw reliable conclusion
Wardlaw et al, 1996	M/A; n = 12 trials, 3435 patients	**Thrombolytic** treatment within 14 days of stroke onset	Possible reduction in disability rate but increase in death rate; use only warranted in context of trials
Blood Pressure in Acute Stroke Collaboration (BASC), 1997	M/A; n = 3 trials, 133 patients	Deliberate alteration of **blood pressure** within two weeks of stroke	Insufficient data to draw any conclusions
Liu et al, 1997	M/A; n = 9 trials, 1214 patients	**Anticoagulation** treatment for >1 months after stroke or transient ischaemic attack	No benefit shown. Appears to be a significant bleeding risk associated with anticoagulant therapy
Bereczki & Fekete, 1997	M/A; n = 1 trial, 33 patients	Use of **vinpocetine** within 14 days of stroke	Insufficient data to draw any conclusions
Counsell & Sandercock, 1998	M/A; n = 5 trials, 501 patients	**Antiplatelet** therapy within 14 days of acute stroke	No benefit shown; insufficient data for certainty (see Table 7.2 for International Stroke Trial Collaborative Group (ISTCG) and Chinese Acute Stroke Trial (CAST))
Liu & Wardlaw, 1998	M/A; n = 8 trials, 1334 patients	Different doses, routes and agents of **thrombolytic** treatment within 14 days of stroke onset	Insufficient evidence to conclude whether lower doses may be safer, or whether any particular agent or route is better than another
Prasad & Shrivastava, 1998	M/A; n = 4 trials, 354 patients	**Surgery** for supratentorial, intra-cerebral haemorrhage, or routine medical care	Insufficient data to draw any conclusions; endoscopic evacuation worth investigation
Qizilbash et al, 1998	M/A; n = 7 trials, 553 patients	Treatment with **corticosteroids**	No benefit shown, wide confidence intervals, expected adverse effects noted
Counsell & Sandercock, 1999	M/A; n = 4 trials, 493 patients	Standard **heparin** or special heparinoid (low molecular weight; LMW)	LMW heparinoid associated with fewer DVTs; data otherwise insufficient to draw conclusions
Gubitz et al, 1999	M/A; n = 21 trials, 23,427 patients	**Anticoagulation** treatment within first two weeks of acute stroke, or not	Reduced rate of DVTs but no other benefit (see Table 8.4 for IST)
Candelise & Ciccone, 1999	M/A; n = 11 trials, 2257 patients	**Ganglioside** treatment within 15 days of onset	Insufficient data to draw reliable conclusion; may cause Guillain-Barre syndrome

Table 7.1 continued

Source	Design & Sample	Intervention(s)	Conclusions
Mohiuddin et al, 1999	M/A; n = 2 trials, 119 patients	**Theophylline** and analogues within seven days of stroke	Insufficient data to draw any conclusions
Ricci, et al 1999	M/A; 3 trials, n = 1002 patients	Use of **piracetam** for acute ischaemic stroke	Possible increase in early death, and no reduction in dependency

DVT Deep vein thrombosis
IST International stroke trial
LMW Low Molecular weight
M/A Meta-analysis

Table 7.2 Specific treatment (drugs and surgery) of acute stroke: other studies

Source	Design & Sample	Intervention(s)	Conclusions
Multi-centre Acute Stroke Trial – Italy (MAST I), 1995	RCT; n = 622 acute stroke patients	**Aspirin** and/or **streptokinase** or placebo	Aspirin alone is beneficial
Mathew et al, 1995	Obs; n = 48 patients with cerebellar haematoma and 71 with posterior fossa (cerebellar) infarction	Conservative management, external **ventricular drainage**, craniectomy and **surgical evacuation** of haemorrhage	Recommended algorithms published. Observe coma and change; drainage initially, evacuate haemorrhage if conscious and has haemorrhage
Goldstein 1995	RCT; n = 96 stroke patients	Observation of patients in pre-existing RCT who were in receipt of **centrally acting drugs** (n = 37) compared with those who were not (n = 59)	Receipt of drugs adversely influenced the degree of upper limb motor control, and independence in ADL
Stroke Prevention in Atrial Fibrillation Investigators, 1996	RCT; n = 1044 patients in atrial fibrillation with at least one embolic risk factor	Adjusted dose **warfarin** vs low-intensity, fixed-dose warfarin + **aspirin**	Adjusted-dose warfarin (target INR 2.0–3.0) importantly reduces stroke for high risk patients
International Stroke Trial Collaborative Group (ISTCG), 1997	RCT; n = 19,435 patients with acute stroke	**Heparin** (subcutaneous) and/or **aspirin** and/or placebo	Heparin offers no benefit; aspirin reduces early recurrence (progress)
Chinese Acute Stroke Trial (CAST), 1997	RCT; n = 21,106 patients, acute stroke	**Aspirin** or placebo	Aspirin reduces risk of death or dependency if given acutely after stroke
Ronning & Guldvog, 1999	CCT*; n = 550 acute stroke patients	**Oxygen 100%,** or air for 24 hours	Higher survival in control group with severe stroke; no other differences

ADL Activities of daily living
CCT Controlled clinical trial (* = quasi-randomised by birth date)
INR International normalised ratio
Obs Observational study
RCT Randomised controlled trial

Table 8.1 Assessment of swallowing after stroke

Source	Design & Sample	Assessment(s)	Conclusions
Splaingard et al, 1988	Obs; n = 107 inpatients in a general rehabilitation hospital (87 adult stroke patients)	Full clinical assessment by speech and language therapistT (40 minutes) against videofluoroscopy assessment (43/107 aspirated)	Clinical assessment of normal swallow: sensitivity 42%, specificity 91%. Significance of silent aspiration unknown
DePippo et al, 1992	Obs; n = 44 'high-risk' patients	Swallow of 80 ml water compared with videofluoroscopy (20/44 abnormal)	Abnormal water swallow in 27; 16 aspirated on video
Kidd et al, 1993	Obs; n = 60 conscious patients within 72 hours of stroke	Swallow of 50 ml water compared with videofluoroscopy (25/60 aspirated)	Abnormal swallow in 25: 20 had aspiration. Abnormal pharyngeal sensation also predicted aspiration
Horner et al, 1993	Obs; n = 38 patients with bilateral stroke (CT scan or MRI scan)	Clinical features compared with video-fluoroscopy (27/38 abnormal)	Abnormal cough and abnormal gag reflex associated with high probability of aspiration (71–93%)
Smithard, et al 1996	Obs; n = 121 acute stroke patients	Standardised bedside assessment of swallowing, and videofluoroscopy	Bedside assessment of swallowing can identify patients at risk of complications as well as videofluoroscopy
Daniels et al, 1998	Obs; n = 55; acute stroke patients, not drowsy	Full clinical assessment compared with videofluoroscopy (21/55 abnormal)	Abnormal voluntary cough and cough on swallow predicted aspiration

CT   Computerised tomography
MRI   Magnetic resonance imaging
Obs   Observational study

Table 8.2 Dysphagia natural history and management

Source	Design & Sample	Intervention(s)	Conclusions
DePippo et al, 1994	RCT; n = 115; patients with mild-moderate dysphagia 3–7 weeks post-stroke	One session explanation and advice, or prescribed diet and monitoring, or diet and therapy	Explanation and advice as effective as more intensive speech and language therapist involvement
Odderson et al, 1995	CCT; n = 124; acute stroke admissions; historical controls	Use of a standardised protocol including dysphagia guidelines	Aspiration pneumonia risk reduced greatly
Teasell et al, 1996	Obs; n = 441; subacute stroke patients in rehabilitation	84 had aspiration on videofluoroscopy; 10/84 aspirators and 2/357 non-aspirators developed pneumonia.	(Silent) aspiration associated with pneumonia
Norton et al, 1996	RCT; n = 30; dysphagia 14 days post-stroke	Percutaneous endoscopic gastrostomy (PEG) feeding or nasogastric tube feeding	PEG associated with better nutrition and better outcome (**NB** many published criticisms)
Garon et al, 1997	RCT; n = 20; 4–17 days post-stroke and aspirating	Thickened fluids alone; or thickened fluids and free access to thin fluids	No additional risk with thin fluids, and possible faster recovery
Perez et al, 1998	RCT; n = 17; patients with dysphagia 2 weeks post-stroke	Nifedipine slow-release 30 mg or placebo	Trend towards improved swallow mechanism in treated group

CCT   Controlled clinical trial
Obs   Observational study
RCT   Randomised controlled trial

Table 8.3 Nutrition after stroke

Source	Design & Sample	Intervention(s)	Conclusions
Potter et al, 1998	M/A; n = 30 trials; 2062 patients, none stroke-specific	Oral or enteral protein supplementation, or normal feeding	Routine supplementation of diet improved nutritional status
Axelsson et al, 1988	Obs; n = 100 acute stroke patients	Observation of nutritional status at admission and discharge	16% of admitted and 22% discharged patients were malnourished
Finestone et al, 1995	Obs; n = 49 patients in stroke rehabilitation service	49% malnourished on admission; had slower rate of recovery	Malnutrition is common and slows recovery
Davalos et al, 1996	Obs; n = 104 acute stroke patients; assessed nutrition and 1 month disability	16% of admitted and 26% of 1 week surviving patients malnourished; outcome worse	Malnutrition is common and worsens in first week; may affect outcome
Reilly, 1996	Obs; n = 150 patients (stroke and non-stroke)	Validation of nutrition risk score between dietitian and nurses	Validated nutritional assessment tool for all ages
Gariballa et al, 1998	Obs; n = 201 acute stroke patients; assessed nutrition and 3 month outcome	20–30% malnourished at admission and further deterioration occurred; serum albumin second only to urine incontinence in predicting poor outcome	Malnutrition is common and worsens in first two weeks; may affect outcome
Penman & Thomson, 1998	*Non-S/R: textured diets for the management of dysphagia*	*Literature review*	*Diverse range of gradings and food texture with no clear criteria for use; SLT and dietetic advice suggested*

M/A   Meta-analysis
Non-S/R Non-systematic review
Obs   Observational study
SLT   Speech and language therapy

Table 8.4 Potential complications of stroke

Source	Design & Sample	Intervention(s)	Conclusions
Antiplatelet Trialists Collaboration (APTC), 1994	M/A; n = 10,000 patients with immobility, mostly surgical	Prolonged antiplatelet therapy (75–325 mg aspirin) as prophylaxis for vascular events	Incidence of DVTs reduced (prevent in 9% of patients) and of PE (prevent in 1.7% of patients)
Wells et al, 1994	*S/R; 12 studies, n = 1842 post-operative moderate risk patients*	*Graduated compression stockings to prevent deep vein thrombosis*	*Use of graduated stockings results in significant risk reduction of DVT after surgery*
Carr & Kenney, 1992	Non-S/R; stroke patients	Review of literature on positioning patients after stroke	Some beneficial positions seemed to be agreed
Lincoln et al, 1996	Obs; n = 76 stroke patients	Observation of care on stroke unit compared with general wards	Patients on the stroke unit had more therapeutic contact with staff and were more often in recommended positions
Chinese Acute Stroke Trial collaborative group (CAST), 1997	RCT; n = 21,106 patients, acute stroke	Aspirin or placebo	No observed difference in pulmonary embolism (only 32 observed, 15 fatal)

▶

Table 8.4 continued

Source	Design & Sample	Intervention(s)	Conclusions
International Stroke Trial Collaborative Group (ISTCG), 1997	RCT; n = 19,435 patients with acute stroke	Heparin (subcutaneous) and/or aspirin and/or placebo	Heparin may reduce overall rate of pulmonary embolism (but study shows no overall benefit)

M/A	Meta-analysis
Non-S/R	Non-systematic review
Obs	Observational study
PE	Pulmonary embolism
RCT	Randomised controlled trial
S/R	Systematic review

Entries in italic denote studies that are not specific to stroke.

Table 8.5 Bladder and bowel management

Source	Design & Sample	Intervention(s)	Conclusions
Shirran & Brazzelli, 1999	S/R; n = 5 RCTs, 345 patients	Review of absorbent products for the containment of urinary and faecal incontinence	Data too few to provide a firm basis for recommendations. New products not tested
Kennedy & Brocklehurst, 1982	*Obs; n = 107 hospitalised and home based patients with indwelling catheters*	*Survey of nursing management of indwelling urinary catheters*	*CSU showed wide range of infections; Catheter by-passing was present in 40%. Some patients were needlessly catheterised*
Kennedy et al, 1983	*Obs; n = 97 elderly hospitalised and home based patients with indwelling catheters*	*Survey of problems associated with in-dwelling urinary catheters: including leaking, blocking, odour and irritation*	*There was an association of large atheters in hospital patients with a higher cnumber of problems, particularly leakage and blocking*
Gelber et al, 1993	Obs; n = 51 stroke patients of whom 19 were incontinent of urine	Urodynamic studies on all 19 incontinent patients	Incontinence was associated with large infarcts. There were three major mechanisms of urinary incontinence
Nakayama et al, 1997	Obs; n = 935 acute stroke patients	Observation of prevalence of urinary (UI) and faecal incontinence (FI) using Barthel subscores during hospital stay and at six months	36% had full UI and 34% full FI at admission. The proportion declined to a fifth UI and a tenth FI by 6 month follow-up
Gross, 1998	Obs; n = 90 incontinent stroke patients in an acute rehabilitation programme	Comparison of the characteristics of those who regained continence to those who did not	50% were continent at discharge. Persisting incontinence was associated with lower total FIM scores and slower progress during rehabilitation
Wikander et al, 1998	CCT; n = 34 incontinent patients in stroke rehabilitation; 21 intervention and 13 controls	Comparison of conventional with FIM governed rehabilitation	20 patients regained continence in FIM governed group compared with 3 in the conventional rehabilitation group

CCT	Controlled clinical trial
CSU	Catheter specimen of urine
FIM	Functional independence measure
Obs	Observational study
S/R	Systematic review

Entries in italic denote studies that are not specific to stroke.

Table 9.1 Epidemiology and treatment of depression after stroke

Source	Design & Sample	Intervention(s)	Conclusions
Lipsey et al, 1984	RCT; n = 39; in- or outpatients with stroke and depression	Nortriptyline compared with placebo in 6 week trial	Eight treated patients withdrawn with complications; reduced level of depression in group tolerating treatment
Reding et al, 1986	RCT; n = 27; inpatients in stroke rehabilitation unit	Trazodone compared with placebo; variable treatment duration, average 32 days	Non-significant trend for Barthel ADL scores to improve more on trazodone. Depression outcomes not reported
Allman et al, 1992	Obs; n = 30 stroke patients (with crying in previous month)	Structured clinical interview to ascertain patterns of crying	No distinct subtypes identified
Andersen et al, 1994	RCT; n = 66 unselected stroke patients 2–52 weeks after stroke	6 weeks citalopram (10–20mg/day) compared with placebo	6 citalopram and 1 placebo patient dropped out. Reduced rate of depression in treated group
Astrom, 1996	Obs; n = 80 acute stroke patients	Assessed for generalised anxiety disorder (GAD) and depression	28% had GAD. Comorbidity with depression was high. Little decrease over 3 years
Raffaele et al, 1996	RCT; n = 22 acute stroke patients	Trazodone 300 mg daily or placebo	Barthel ADL index improved with trazodone in patients with abnormal dexamethasone suppression test
Dam et al, 1996	RCT; n = 52 patients 1–6 months post-stroke; unable to walk	Fluoxetine, maprotiline or placebo for 3 months	Fluoxetine associated with better functional outcome; depression no different
Schultz et al, 1997	Obs; n = 142 stroke patients	2 years evaluation of depressive symptoms at 3, 6, 12 and 24 months	Anxiety was associated with increased severity of depressive symptoms and greater impairment in function. Women and younger patients reported more symptoms
Palomaki et al, 1999	RCT; n = 100 acute stroke patients aged under 71 years	Mianserin 60 mg daily, or placebo; seen at 2, 6, 12, 18 months	No difference in depression, or ADL independence; low rate of depression (6–16%). Routine mianserin not indicated

ADL   Activities of daily living
Obs   Observational study
RCT   Randomised controlled trial

Table 9.2 Treating emotionalism

Source	Design & Sample	Intervention(s)	Conclusions
Lawson & MacLeod 1969	*RCT; n = 7; subjects with organic emotionalism, not all stroke*	*Imipramine 10 mg, imipramine 20 mg, phenobarbitone and placebo compared in a crossover design*	*Imipramine in both doses, but not phenobarbitone or placebo, reduced crying and laughing*
Schiffer et al, 1985	*RCT; n = 12; patients with multiple sclerosis*	*Amitriptyline compared with placebo using crossover design*	*Amitriptyline more effective than placebo in reducing crying*
Andersen et al, 1993	RCT; n = 16; subjects 6 days to >2 years after stroke	Citalopram and placebo compared in a crossover design	Citalopram reduced rate of crying more than placebo, in a 3 week trial.
Robinson et al, 1993	RCT; n = 28; emotionalism after stroke	Nortriptyline compared with placebo	Nortriptyline more effective than placebo in reducing crying. Only one drop-out
Brown et al, 1998	CCT; n = 20 patients with emotionalism after stroke	Fluoxetine for post-stroke emotionalism	Clinically significant improvement from 3rd day of treatment

CCT   Controlled clinical trial
RCT   Randomised controlled trial
Entries in italic denote studies that are not specific to stroke

Table 9.3 Treating cognitive deficits (including visual field retraining)

Source	Design & Sample	Intervention(s)	Conclusions
Lincoln et al, 1985	RCT; n = 33; head injury or stroke (n = 27) with neglect	Perceptual training or conventional occupational therapy	No difference in outcome (trend to help on some tests)
Gray et al, 1992	RCT; n = 31 acute brain injury (including stroke) with attentional deficit	Computerised attentional retraining (17) or recreational computing (14)	Cognitive impairment less late but not immediately after attention retraining
Kerkhoff et al, 1994	CCT; n = 22 patients with long-term hemianopia	Saccadic eye movement training	Long-term reduction in field defects with functional gains
Kalra et al 1997	RCT; n = 50 patients with visual neglect after stroke	Conventional therapy vs spatiomotor cueing and early emphasis on restoration of function	Intervention group had significantly shorter length of stay and higher Barthel ADL index scores (not significant)
Lincoln et al, 1997	RCT; n = stroke patients	Randomly allocated to stroke unit or general ward. Perceptual impairment measured at 3, 6 and 12 months after randomisation	Stroke unit patients showed significantly less impairment of perceptual abilities at all stages of stroke

ADL   Activities of daily living
CCT   Controlled clinical trial
RCT   Randomised controlled trial

Table 9.4 Management of dysphasia

Source	Design & Sample	Intervention(s)	Conclusions
Whurr et al, 1992	M/A; n = 45 studies; n = 1,336 patients with aphasia	Speech therapy treatment	Effect of treatment shown (but not all studies were RCTs)
Robey, 1998	M/A; n = 55 studies; n = 1491 patients with aphasia	Speech therapy treatment	Effect of treatment shown (but not all studies were RCTs)
Greener et al, 1999	M/A; 12 trials; n = 1254 adults with aphasia as a result of stroke	Speech and language therapy by trained therapist in any setting	SLT shown to be neither effective nor ineffective
Wertz et al, 1981	RCT; n = 67 stroke patients with aphasia	Group therapy or individual therapy; 8 hours/week for weeks 4–48 post-stroke	Most measures no different; both groups improved; only difference in one measure favouring individual therapy
David et al, 1982	RCT; n = 96 stroke patients with aphasia	Assessment, then treatment by volunteer or therapist	No difference in outcome; assessment improved communication
Wertz et al, 1986	RCT; n = 121 patients with acute aphasia 2–24 weeks post-onset	Assessment, then: immediate therapy from therapist, delayed therapy from therapist; or immediate therapy from volunteer	Patients improve naturally; treatment improved rate and extent of recovery; delaying treatment did not affect outcome; therapy from trained volunteers as effective as from therapists
Rice et al,1987	Obs; n = 10 carers of aphasic adults	Support group	Good attenders showed improvement on measures of social dysfunction, and psychological well-being
Bruce & Howard, 1987	CCT; n = 5 patients with Broca's aphasia who could respond to phonemic cues from a therapist	Computer-generated phonemic cues	4 cases were better at naming and indicating 1st letters of items
Poeck et al, 1989	CCT; n = 68 inpatients with aphasia resulting from injury of vascular origin	Intensive language treatment 9 hours per week for 6–8 weeks. Three groups: early, late and control	Improvement (in 78% treated up to 4 months post-onset; and 46% of those treated 4–12 months post-onset) beyond 'what would be expected from spontaneous recovery'
Brindley et al, 1989	CCT; n = 10 patients with chronic aphasia	Intensive therapy over 4 weeks	Improvement in communication occurred
Mackenzie, 1991	CCT; n = 5 patients with chronic aphasia	Intensive and group therapy	Improvement in communication occurred, but not maintained
Katz & Wertz, 1997	RCT; n = 55 patients with chronic aphasia	Computer reading programme, stimulation or nil	Specific computer-based treatment improves reading
Lyon et al, 1997	Obs; n = 10 aphasic adults	Community volunteers	Subjective improvements in well-being

M/A   Meta-analysis
CCT   Controlled clinical trial
Obs   Observational study
RCT   Randomised controlled trial

Table 9.5 Technologically assisted feedback including biofeedback
(*Studies in meta-analyses also included in table*)

Source	Design & Sample	Intervention(s)	Conclusions
Schleenbaker & Mainous, 1993	M/A; n = 8 trials, 192 patients	Biofeedback, arm or leg	Biofeedback may be useful, but unproven
Moreland & Thomson, 1994	M/A; n = 5 trials, 135 patients	Biofeedback relating to arm	No difference in outcome between biofeedback and conventional therapy
Glanz et al, 1995	M/A; n = 8 trials, 168 patients post-acute stroke	Biofeedback (arm or leg)	Efficacy of biofeedback not established; insufficient data
Moreland et al, 1998	M/A; n = 8 trials	EMG biofeedback from leg, no or conventional therapy	EMG biofeedback increased ankle dorsiflexion strength (but little else)
Basmajian et al, 1975	RCT; n = 20 patients with footdrop following stroke 3+ months ago	Therapy with/without additional EMG biofeedback, over 5 weeks	Addition of BFB facilitated recovery from impairments
Lee et al, 1976	RCT; n = 18 patients with weak deltoid	True, false or absent biofeedback from deltoid muscle	No effect on strength of voluntary muscle contraction
Bowman et al, 1979	RCT; n = 30 stroke patients, recent onset	Positional feedback and muscle stimulation (PFST) to weak wrist, or routine therapy	Wrist extension strength greatly increased by PFST
Smith, 1979	RCT; n = 11 chronic stroke patients	EMG biofeedback on arm, 12 sessions in 6 weeks	More improvement, but not statistically significant
Greenberg & Fowler, 1980	RCT; n = 20 patients with some arm movement 1+ years post-onset	Normal occupational therapy, or audio-feedback on elbow extension	Both groups increased elbow extension; no differences between groups; biofeedback not helpful
Hurd et al, 1980	RCT; n = (a) 24 rehabilitation patients; and (b) 20 patients	(a) real or sham EMG biofeedback; (b) random muscle selection deltoid/anterior tibial	Possible effect to specific muscle targeted; functional change not assessed
Prevo et al, 1982	RCT; n = 18 chronic stroke patients	EMG biofeedback on arm, 28 sessions in 11 weeks	No benefit noted
Burnside et al, 1982	CCT; n = 22 patients late after stroke	EMG biofeedback or routine therapy for weak leg	EMG associated with greater and more sustained improvements
Basmajian et al, 1982	RCT; n = 37 stroke patients	EMG biofeedback or physiotherapy exercises	Minor differences
Winchester et al, 1983	RCT; n = 40 adult hemiparetic patients	Feedback stimulation training and electrical stimulation	Increased knee extension torque, but control no better
Inglis et al, 1984	RCT; n = 30 stroke patients six months post-stroke: (crossover after treatment)	Physiotherapy ± additional EMG biofeedback in arm muscles	Some possible minor additional benefit from EMG biofeedback
John, 1986	RCT; n = 12 patients 12 weeks post-stroke	Additional EMG biofeedback on leg muscles	No additional benefit from biofeedback

Table 9.5 (continued)

Source	Design & Sample	Intervention(s)	Conclusions
Cozean et al, 1988	RCT; n = 36 acute stroke patients	Physiotherapy/EMG biofeedback/ FES/BFB and FES	Combined treatment of BFB and FES improved gait most
Crow et al, 1989	RCT; n = 40 acute stroke patients	Real or placebo EMG biofeedback on arm muscles	Biofeedback improved speed of recovery, especially in severe impairment
Mandel et al, 1990	RCT; n = 37 stroke patients, 6+ months post-stroke	No therapy/biofeedback/rhythm and biofeedback	Gait improved with biofeedback; rhythmic pacing led to sustained improvement in gait
Svensson et al, 1992	RCT; n = 35 patients with facial palsy	Facial muscle retraining using EMG feedback	No benefits observed
Morris et al, 1992	RCT; n = 26 patients with knee hyperextension	EMG biofeedback added to conventional therapy	EMG biofeedback enhanced reduction of knee hyperextension
Colborne et al, 1993	RCT; n = 8 patients 6+ months post-stroke	Physiotherapy/EMG biofeedback on ankle angle	Both feedback methods improved gait
Wolf et al, 1994	RCT; n = 16 patients 1+ years post-stroke	EMG biofeedback to strengthen weak triceps	Both groups increased strength, no difference
Montoya et al, 1994	CCT; n = 16 patients post-rehabilitation	Visual stimulation on step length with feedback	Asymmetry reduced; step length increased
Intiso et al, 1994	RCT; n = 16 stroke patients late post-stroke	Biofeedback on ankle dorsiflexion muscles	Ankle dorsiflexion increased
Sukthankar et al, 1994	*RCT; n = 12 patients; head injury or stroke*	*Biofeedback on force of selected oral movements*	*Feedback increased control of oral muscles*
Fanthome et al, 1995	RCT; n = 18; right hemisphere stroke with 'neglect'	Feedback on eye movements into 'neglected' visual field	No effect on neglect (eye movements may possibly have altered)
Dursun et al, 1996	CCT; n = 37 acute stroke patients	Physiotherapy (2.5 hours/day) + feedback on sitting balance or additional 30 min physiotherapy	Feedback on sitting balance speeded recovery of balance and walking; hospital length of stay shorter
Wong et al, 1997	RCT; n = 60 stroke (55) or head injury (5) patients with hemiplegia	Balance retraining by visual and auditory feedback or standard balance training	Stance symmetry improved greatly, and group difference maintained
Sackley & Lincoln, 1997	RCT; n = 26; 4–63 weeks post-stroke	Balance retraining by visual feedback	More rapid recovery of balance and reduction in disability, end result same
Bradley et al, 1998	RCT; n = 21 patients with acute stroke	Additional EMG feedback or sham EMG feedback	No differences in mobility outcome

BFB   Biofeedback
CCT   Controlled clinical trial
EMG   Electromyography (recording of electrical potential from contracting muscle)
FES   Functional electrical stimulation
M/A   Meta-analysis (and systematic review)
RCT   Randomised controlled trial
Entries in italic denote studies that are not specific to stroke

Table 9.6 Functional electrical stimulation (FES)

Source	Design & Sample	Intervention(s)	Conclusions
Glanz et al, 1996	M/A; n = 4 trials, 132 patients	Electrostimulation +/− biofeedback	FES decreases motor impairment (increases strength)
Cozean et al, 1988	RCT; n = 36 acute stroke patients	Physiotherapy/EMG biofeedback/FES/BFB and FES	Combined treatment of BFB and FES improved gait most
Faghri et al, 1994	RCT; n = 26 patients	Routine physiotherapy ± additional FES to shoulder	Some benefits from FES on range of movement
Faghri & Rodgers, 1997	RCT; n = 26 patients with shoulder weakness post-stroke	Routine therapy ± functional neuromuscular stimulation (FNS) to deltoid	Improved active and passive range of motion with FNS
Burridge et al, 1997	RCT; n = 16 patients with chronic hemiplegia	Odstock dropped foot stimulator (ODFS) or physiotherapy alone	ODFS improved gait while used, but not once stopped
Chae et al, 1998	RCT; n = 46 (28 complete) within 4 weeks of stroke	Functional electrical stimulation of wrist extensors, or minor skin stimulation	More motor recovery with FES, but many dropped out with pain/discomfort
Linn et al, 1999	RCT; n = 40 acute stroke patients	FES around shoulder, or no FES (not blinded)	Subluxation less immediately after FES; but no carryover; 12 week outcome no different
Powell et al, 1999	RCT; n = 60 acute stroke patients	FES for wrist extension, or no FES (not blinded), for eight weeks	Increased strength wrist extension, grip and grasp at 8 weeks but not at 32 weeks; most effect in patients with some movement

BFB   Biofeedback
EMG   Electromyography (recording of electrical potential from contracting muscle)
FES   Functional electrical stimulation
M/A   Meta-analysis
RCT   Randomised controlled trial

Table 9.7 Spasticity

Source	Design & Sample	Intervention(s)	Conclusions
Burt & Currie, 1978	RCT; n = 28 (initially 44), 2–27 months post-stroke	Baclofen or diazepam	Both drugs reduced spasticity; baclofen improved gait
Ketel & Kolb, 1984	CCT; n = 14; stroke patients with spasticity limiting rehabilitation	Change from dantrolene to placebo	Increased deficits on withdrawal of active drug; dantrolene beneficial
Medici et al, 1989	RCT; n = 30; stroke patients with spasticity	Tizanidine or baclofen, titrated dosage	Both reduced spasticity, slight favour for tizanidine
Katrak et al, 1992	RCT; n = 31; acute stroke, before spasticity	Dantrolene 200 mg/day or placebo	No benefits observed with routine use of dantrolene
Beckerman et al, 1996a,b	RCT; n = 60 acute stroke patients	AFO/PAFO, and thermocoagulation of tibial nerve or placebo coagulation	Thermocoagulation reduced spasticity but no benefit; AFO had no effect

Table 9.7 continued

Source	Design & Sample	Intervention(s)	Conclusions
Miller & Light, 1997	CCT; n = 9 patients with spastic left arm	Graded restive exercises given	No increase in spasticity; some decrease in contraction
Sharp & Brouwer, 1997	CCT; n = 15 patients 6+ months post-stroke	40 minutes/day, 3 days/week, 6 weeks leg strengthening programme	Programme improved gait and strength without causing increase in spasticity
Brown & Kautz, 1998	CCT; n = 15; stroke >6 months post-stroke	Random variation in leg workload	No additional inappropriate muscle activity with exercise
Ada et al,1998	Obs; n = 14 stroke patients and 15 neurologically normal controls	Measurement of resting and action reflexes of gastronemius muscle in conditions that simulated walking	Spasticity does not cause problems for ambulant patients' walking after stroke. It is inappropriate routinely to inhibit the reflex response to improve functional movement

AFO   Ankle-foot orthosis
CCT   Controlled clinical trial
Obs   Observational study
PAFO Placebo ankle foot orthosis
RCT   Randomised controlled trial

Table 9.8 Botulinum toxin and spasticity

Source	Design & Sample	Intervention(s)	Conclusions
Snow et al, 1990	RCT; n = 9 patients with stable multiple sclerosis	Botulinum toxin or placebo into adductor muscles	Toxin reduced spasticity and improved hygiene
Grazko et al, 1995	RCT; n = 12 patients with spasticity (3 with stroke)	Botulinum toxin into spastic muscles (no EMG guidance)	Botulinum toxin always reduced spasticity, for 2–4 months. Function often improved
Hesse et al, 1996a	CCT; n = 12; leg spasticity 11+ months after stroke	Botulinum toxin into leg muscles; selective placement with EMG guidance	Improved gait in 9 out of the 12 patients
Simpson et al, 1996	RCT; n = 39; patients with arm spasticity 9+ months after stroke	Various doses of botulinum toxin, including placebo	Tone was reduced by botulinum toxin
Bhakta et al, 1996	CCT; n = 17; over one year after stroke; spastic arm	Botulinum toxin in various arm muscles	Wide range of benefits, including in mobility, lasting one to eleven months
Burbaud et al, 1996	RCT; n = 23; patients with spastic leg after stroke	Botulinum toxin or placebo; crossover at 90 days	Botulinum toxin improved gait speed and reduced spasticity
Childers et al, 1996	RCT; n = 17; patients with chronic hemiplegia after stroke	Botulinum toxin in one of two sites in calf (gastrocnemius): mid calf or proximal calf	Injection to mid-calf no different from injection near muscle origin; site unimportant
Sampaio et al, 1997	CCT; n = 19; patients over 6 months post-stroke with spastic arms	Botulinum toxin into forearm muscles	Function improved and spasticity reduced after injection

▶

Table 9.8 continued

Source	Design & Sample	Intervention(s)	Conclusions
Corry et al, 1997	*RCT; n = 14; children with cerebral palsy and hemiplegia in arm*	*Botulinum toxin or saline intra-muscularly*	*Botulinum increased active movement and some functions, and decreased tone and associated movements*
Reiter et al, 1998	RCT; n = 18; stroke outpatients with spastic foot 10+ months post-stroke	Botulinum toxin to calf with EMG guidance, or lower dose to tibialis posterior (no EMG guidance) with strapping for 3 weeks	Both groups walked better; no major differences observed; EMG-guided injection not especially better.
Hesse et al, 1998	RCT; n = 24, 6–11 months post- stroke	Botulinum or placebo; electrical stimulation or not; into arm flexor muscles	Botulinum toxin with additional stimulation at times increased effect of toxin and reduced disability
Corry et al, 1998	*RCT; n = 20 children with cerebral palsy and spastic equines*	*Botulinum toxin or serial plaster casts*	*Equally effective; some possible advantages for botulinum toxin*

CCT   Controlled clinical trial
EMG   Electromyography (recording of electrical potential from contracting muscle)
RCT   Randomised controlled trial
Entries in italic denote studies that are not specific to stroke.

Table 9.9 Sensory impairment and post-stroke pain

Source	Design & Sample	Intervention(s)	Conclusions
Wiffen et al, 1999	*M/A; 20 trials, 746 patients with acute and chronic pain (some stroke)*	*Evaluation of the analgesic effectiveness of anticonvulsant drugs*	*Carbamazepine little effect in post-stroke pain. Antidepressants may be better but more trials are needed*
Leijon & Boivie 1989	CCT with crossover; n = 15 patients with post-stroke pain	Amitriptyline vs carbamazepine vs placebo	Amitriptyline produced statistically significant reduction of pain compared with placebo. The effect of Carbamazepine was not significant
Yekutiel & Guttman, 1993	CCT; n = 39; stroke patients with sensory loss 2 years post-stroke	Sensory re-education, 45 min, 3x/week, 6 weeks	Sensory ability improved (effect on function not assessed)

CCT   Controlled clinical trial
M/A   Meta-analysis
Entries in italic denote studies that are not specific to stroke.

Table 9.10 Shoulder pain after stroke

Source	Design & Sample	Intervention(s)	Conclusions
Partridge et al, 1990	RCT; n = 65 patients with post-stroke shoulder pain	Cryotherapy or Bobath physiotherapy	No significant differences in pain outcome; both improved equally
Kumar et al, 1990	RCT; n = 28; patients in stroke rehabilitation unit	Physical range of motion; skate-board RoM; overhead pulley RoM	Overhead pulley caused shoulder pain
Leandri et al, 1990	RCT; n = 60; patients with hemiplegic shoulder pain	Transcutaneous electrical nerve stimulation (TENS) at intensity: zero, low, high	High intensity TENS led to prolonged pain relief and increase in RoM
Kotzki et al, 1991	RCT; n = 42; stroke rehabilitation unit patients	Postural support and functional electrical stimulation; foam support; (Bobath) pillow support	Foam support (+/– FES) was more effective at preventing shoulder pain than Bobath pillow
Ancliffe, 1992	CCT (alternating allocation); n = 8; patients admitted to hospital	Strapping of shoulder or no strapping	Strapping associated with many more days without pain
Braus et al, 1994	CCT; n = 86 patients with shoulder-hand syndrome after stroke	Instructions to everyone, including family, on handling arm	Shoulder-hand syndrome reduced from 27% to 8%
Wanklyn et al, 1996	Obs; n = 108 stroke patients	Follow-up for 6 months after discharge from hospital for hemiplegic shoulder pain (HSP)	63.8% developed HSP during study period. Prevalence increased in 1st weeks after discharge from hospital. Patients and carers need advice about correct handling of the hemiplegic arm
Dekker et al, 1997	RCT (single-case design, random start time); n = 7; stroke and shoulder pain	Three 40 mg intra-articular triamcinolone on days 1, 8, 22 after start time	Five of seven responded with reduction in pain, and four had improved range of movement
Linn et al, 1999	RCT; n = 40 acute stroke patients	FES around shoulder, or no FES (not blinded)	Subluxation less immediately after FES; but no carryover; 12 week outcome no different
Chantraine et al, 1999	CCT; n = 120 patients with subluxed painful shoulder	Alternate allocation to additional FES	Pain less; subluxation less; motor recovery better

CCT Controlled clinical trial
FES Functional electrical stimulation
Obs Observational study
RCT Randomised controlled trial
RoM Range of movement (or motion)

Table 9.11 Studies on TENS and acupuncture

Source	Design & Sample	Intervention(s)	Conclusions
Johansson et al, 1993	RCT; n = 78 acute stroke patients	Additional acupuncture twice weekly for 10 weeks	Additional acupuncture improved outcome
Hu et al, 1993	RCT; n = 30 acute stroke patients	Additional acupuncture three times weekly, four weeks	Acupuncture improved outcome, which was maintained
Sallstrom et al, 1996	RCT; n = 45 acute stroke patients	Additional acupuncture four times weekly for six weeks	Acupuncture improved outcome, including quality of life
Kjendahl et al, 1997	RCT; n = 41 acute stroke patients	Additional acupuncture (traditional Chinese approach) for six weeks	Additional acupuncture improved outcome in short- and long-term
Gosman-Hedstrom et al, 1998	RCT; n = 104 acute stroke patients	Acupuncture twice weekly for 10 weeks: deep, or superficial, or none	No differences seen in recovery of motor impairment or ADL
Tekeoolu et al, 1998	RCT; n = 60 patients sub-acute stroke	TENS or placebo-TENS	Greater increase in independence following TENS
Sonde et al, 1998	RCT; n = 44 patients 6–12 months post-stroke with weak arm	Routine therapy ± low-frequency (1.7 Hz) TENS to weak arm	Motor control increased if some present initially; spasticity and pain unaffected

ADL   Activities of daily living
Hz   Hertz (cycles per second)
RCT   Randomised controlled trial
TENS Transcutaneous electrical nerve stimulation

Table 9.12 Drugs directly reducing impairment/disability

Source	Design & Sample	Intervention(s)	Conclusions
West & Stockel, 1965	RCT; n = 29 people with post-stroke aphasia	**Meprobamate** or placebo; with speech therapy	No benefit observed
Sarno et al, 1972	RCT; n = 16 people with aphasia 3+ months post-stroke	**Hyperbaric oxygen:** 100% oxygen vs air at 2 atmospheres	No benefit on communication observed
Crisostomo et al, 1988	RCT; n = 8 acute stroke patients	**Amphetamine** (10 mg) or placebo once only; with physiotherapy	Motor recovery in subsequent therapy session greatly enhanced
Enderby et al, 1994	RCT; n = 137 acute stroke patients (67 with aphasia)	**Piracetam** 4.8 grams/day for 12 weeks	Level of aphasia reduced more in piracetam group over 12 weeks; no other differences seen
Walker-Batson et al, 1995	RCT; n = 10 patients; 16–30 days after stroke	**Amphetamine** (10 mg) or placebo, every 4 days ×10; both with physiotherapy	Rate and extent of motor recovery enhanced and sustained 1 year
Goldstein, 1995	Obs; n = 96 acute stroke patients	Association between **centrally acting**, 'detrimental' drugs and outcome	Patients receiving detrimental drugs (eg benzodiazepines) did less well

Table 9.12 continued

Source	Design & Sample	Intervention(s)	Conclusions
Gupta et al, 1995	RCT; n = 20 patients with aphasia 13–200 months post-stroke	**Bromocriptine** up to 15mg/day or placebo	No benefits observed
Sabe et al, 1995	RCT; n = 7 patients with aphasia more than one year	**Bromocriptine** up to 60mg/day or placebo	No benefits observed
Dam et al, 1996	RCT; n = 52 patients 1–6 months post-stroke; unable to walk	**Fluoxetine, maprotiline** or placebo for 3 months	Fluoxetine associated with better functional outcome; depression no different
Huber et al, 1997	RCT; n = 66 patients with acute aphasia	**Piracetam** 4.8 grams/day or placebo	Trend for greater improvement with piracetam
Grade et al, 1998	RCT; n = 21 patients soon after stroke	**Methylphenidate** 30 mg daily, or placebo; full rehabilitation programme	Drug reduced depression and increased functional recovery
Miyai & Reding, 1998	RCT; n = 24 depressed patients	**Desipramine, trazadone or fluoxetine** for four weeks	Serotonergic drugs associated with better functional recovery; no differences on depression

Obs   Observational study
RCT   Randomised controlled trial

Table 9.13 Gait re-training: treadmill use, and other studies

Source	Design & Sample	Intervention(s)	Conclusions
Wall & Turnbull, 1987	RCT; n = 20 patients late after stroke	Outpatient Bobath or home-based Bobath	Both groups improved; no differences
Mandel et al, 1990	RCT; n = 37 stroke patients	Routine/biofeedback/rhythm and biofeedback	Rhythmic pacing led to improved gait
Richards et al, 1993 (see also Malouin et al, 1992)	RCT; n = 27 acute stroke patients	Early, intensive conventional therapy; later less intensive conventional therapy; early intensive gait and muscle retraining	Early muscle retraining and gait retraining (on treadmill) facilitated gait recovery; no differences between conventional groups
Montoya et al, 1994	RCT; n = 16 patients with stroke	Treadmill training, ± feedback of length of stride, aiming for lighted target	Training to increase stride length lengthened stride
Hesse et al, 1994	CCT; n = 9 patients 8+ weeks post-stroke with static gait ability	Treadmill training with partial bodyweight support	Further improvement in gait follows treadmill training
Hesse et al, 1995a, b	CCT; n = 7 patients 3+ months post-stroke	Treadmill training and Bobath physiotherapy	Treadmill training improved gait, Bobath physiotherapy did not
Schauer et al, 1996	CCT; n = 6 patients with gait disability	Music	Music decreased gait asymmetry

▶

Table 9.13 continued

Source	Design & Sample	Intervention(s)	Conclusions
Macko et al, 1997	Obs; n = 9 patients with long-standing stroke	Treadmill training for 6 months	Low-intensity training improved cardiovascular fitness
Thaut et al, 1997	RCT; n = 20 patients as soon as took 5 steps	Rhythmic auditory stimulation, or normal (Bobath); 1 hour daily, 5 days/week, 6 weeks	Rhythmic auditory stimulation (music with beat) led to more and sustained improvement in gait
Visintin et al, 1998	RCT; n = 100 patients with acute stroke	Treadmill gait training with 40% or 0% weight carried by harness	Partial support during training led to better gait, and a sustained advantage

CCT   Controlled clinical trial
Obs   Observational study
RCT   Randomised controlled trial

Table 9.14 Equipment (assistive devices)

Source	Design & Sample	Intervention(s)	Conclusions
Smith et al, 1981b	Obs; n = 311 stroke patients in RCT	Stroke unit patients given more aids (582 vs 325) and used more at one year (295 vs 165); use of aids declined over year; frequency: mobility > hygiene > feeding > dressing > rest	Organised care (as recommended) associated with provision and continued use of more aids and equipment
Chamberlain et al, 1981	RCT; n = 100 patients leaving hospital needing bath aids	Immediate provision of aids and instruction by occupational therapy (OT) vs usual service	At 3–6 months OT home visit significantly increased the use of bathing aids and level satisfaction to 90–100%
Bynum & Rogers, 1987	Obs; n = 30 home-care recipients	Assessment of effectiveness of 54 devices	82% used; non-use due to functional improvement and faulty prescription
Borello-France et al, 1988	CCT; n = 41 acute stroke patients	Wheelchair: normal; with seat board; with seat board and back board. Eight weeks	Posture altered by boards, but no effect on posture remained after removal of boards
George et al, 1988	Obs; n = 140 elderly (random sample from GP register)	Assessment of use of aids and home adaptations	50% non-use, also significant number needing additional aids. GPs should screen for use
Gardner et al, 1993	Obs; n = 28 aids; survey and expert opinion	Appraisal of 28 aids directly available to public	Many products inadequate; some could be hazardous in older people's homes
Gitlin et al, 1993	Obs; n = 13 patients (4 with stroke) and 72 devices issued	31–39% never used, 41–57% always used	Needs and use varied widely, and over time. Need to assess and train in home with carer
Neville et al, 1993	Obs; general patients, after-hospital discharge	Quality assurance study	85% utilisation (but 22% non-response); need for retrieval system, for personal and environmental assessment
Mann et al, 1995	Obs; n = 30 stroke subjects aged over 60, at home	Assessment of assistive device needs	Need for additional devices, lack of up-to-date information about availability

Table 9.14 Equipment (assistive devices)

Source	Design & Sample	Intervention(s)	Conclusions
Gladman et al, 1995	Obs; n = 162 stroke patients at home	Median (interquartile range) 3 (1–5) treatments after discharge teaching use of equipment/aids	Need to devote significant resources to assessing and teaching about aids at home after stroke
Hass et al, 1996	Obs; n = 38/156 patients 15 months post-stroke	From 156, 120 asked, 102 replied, 56 used equipment, 38 seen	Mobility equipment was the most common: 82/92 pieces
Gitlin et al, 1996	*Obs; n = 86 patients (28 stroke) and 642 devices*	*32% devices for mobility, 30% for dressing, 26% for bathing. Only about 50% used always, 47% never used*	*Pattern of use established in 4 weeks; 20% of stroke patients only used device short-term*
Sonn et al, 1996	*Obs; n = 170 community based people over 70 years of age*	*Assessment of usage rate and effectiveness of equipment 6, 12 months post-prescription*	*Usage rate 84%, non-use due to changed health status; need follow-up over time*
Hesse et al, 1996b	Obs; n = 194 stroke patients; German rehabilitation centre	Questionnaire 6–10 months after discharge about use of aids/assistive devices	85% satisfied over 50% level; need to consider ability of user and environment; more home visits may be useful
Huck & Bonhotal, 1997	RCT; n = 10 stroke patients	Type and location of fastener studied (factorial block design study)	Velcro fastener centre front was best and preferred option
Gitlin et al, 1998	Obs; n = 103 stroke patients at end of rehabilitation; 823 devices	Structured, qualitative approach to establish concerns	Six areas: operation of device; utility of device; social contexts; personal meaning of using device; learning to use device; and (hope) that it is transitory
Mann et al, 1999	*RCT; n = 104 home-based frail elderly persons (not only stroke)*	*Assistive devices, and environmental changes to maintain independence as required vs 'usual care services'*	*In the intervention group decline was slowed, and costs for domiciliary care staff and institutional care were lower; total cost lower in intervention group*

CCT   Controlled clinical trial
GP   General practitioner (family doctor)
Obs   Observational study
RCT   Randomised controlled trial
Entries in italic denote studies that are not specific to stroke.

Table 9.15 Ankle-foot orthoses

Source	Design & Sample	Intervention(s)	Conclusions
Corcoran et al, 1970	RCT; n = 15 patients 6+ months post-stroke	Metal or plastic AFO, or neither	AFOs increased speed and efficiency of gait
Beckerman et al, 1996a	RCT; n = 60 acute stroke patients	AFO/PAFO, and thermocoagulation of tibial nerve or placebo coagulation	Thermocoagulation reduced spasticity, but no benefit; AFO had no effect
Beckerman et al, 1996b	RCT; n = 60 acute stroke patients	AFO/PAFO, and thermocoagulation of tibial nerve or placebo coagulation	AFO and thermocoagulation, individually or combined, did not improve walking

AFO   Ankle-foot orthosis
PAFO Placebo Ankle-foot orthosis
RCT   Randomised controlled trial

Table 9.16 Walking aids

Source	Design & Sample	Intervention(s)	Conclusion
Waldron & Bohannon, 1989	CCT; n = 20 ambulatory stroke patients 130 days post-stroke	The effect of changing cane conditions on weight-bearing ratio	Using a cane did not lead to greater weight-bearing asymmetry
Tyson & Ashburn, 1994	CCT; n = 20 ambulatory stroke patients 27.6 months post-stroke	The effect of changing cane conditions on the gait cycle	Walking aids had no effect in 'good walkers' but in 'poor walkers' they had a beneficial effect on gait
Lu et al, 1997	CCT; n = 10 late post-stroke patients	Length of walking stick (to greater trochanter or wrist crease) and gait stability and speed	Wrist crease stick better than stick to greater trochanter
Tyson et al, 1998	CCT; n = 20 ambulatory stroke patients 27.6 months post-stroke	The effect of changing cane conditions on support taken from the cane on the gait cycle	Different types of aid did not influence the amount of support taken by hemiplegic patients

CCT   Controlled clinical trial

Table 10.1 Discharge planning

Source	Design & Sample	Intervention(s)	Conclusions
Early Supported Discharge Trialists, 1999	M/A; 9 trials; n = about 400 selected elderly stroke patients	Early discharge with community-based rehabilitation from specialist team	Early supported discharge can reduce length of stay for selected patients. The relative risks and benefits and overall costs remain unclear
Campion et al, 1983	CCT; n = 132 acute geriatric admissions	Geriatric consultation service in one ward; not in two	Increased use of rehabilitation services three times; no effect on LoS, re-admissions or discharge placement
Ebrahim et al, 1987	Obs; n = 183 patients at home at 6 months	Audit of follow-up	30% had not seen GP; under half had aids for extant problems Planning and follow-up may be sub-optimal
Kennedy et al, 1987 Neidlinger et al, 1987	RCT; n = 80 elderly acute admissions	Special nurse with special discharge protocol; or normal services	Reduced length of stay (2 days out of 10); less readmission. Cost-effectiveness shown
Victor & Vetter, 1988	Obs; n = 1930 patients 3 months after being discharged	Questionnaire on discharge planning	Under 50% had any discussion of needs prior to discharge; 40% had less than 24 hours notice, but only 25% dissatisfied
Glennon & Smith, 1990	Obs; 46 case conferences, 45 patients, 213 questions	Record of questions asked by patient or family	Questions on discharge planning second most common (16%)
Naylor, 1990	RCT; n = 40 elderly patients	Comprehensive discharge planning protocol for elderly implemented by special nurse	Fewer readmissions, initial length of stay unchanged
Mamon et al, 1992	Obs; n = 919 discharges	Association between use or not of a single discharge co-ordinator	With a single person responsible, there were fewer unmet treatment needs at discharge, but care needs still unmet
Evans & Hendricks, 1993	RCT; n = 835 'high-risk' admissions	Discharge planning from day 3 of admission	Discharge planning increased discharge home, reduced readmission rate and total hospital stay, but did not affect initial length of stay
Naylor et al, 1994	RCT; n = 276 patients aged 70+ years with heart disease (medical) or heart surgery (surgical)	Comprehensive discharge planning protocol for elderly, executed by nurse specialist	Protocol led to shorter admission and fewer readmissions in medical (but not surgical) patients. Was cost-effective
Parfrey et al, 1994	RCT; n = 1599 acute patients (2 hospitals)	Questionnaire to identify patients for referral to professions	Shorter length of stay in one hospital; identification of patients needing help possible using questionnaire
Charles et al, 1994	Obs; n = 4599 patients seen after discharge	Interview to establish areas of dissatisfaction with hospital care	30–40% had complaints about discharge process; biggest area of dissatisfaction
Landefeld et al, 1995	RCT; n = 651 acutely ill hospital admissions aged 70+	Routine care, or special unit with (a) good environment, (b) patient-centred care with protocols, (c) discharge planning, (d) specialist medical input	Specialised unit reduced dependence and discharge to nursing home
Wei et al, 1995	Obs; n = 20,136 discharged patients aged 65 years or more	Relationship between factors documented at discharge and mortality or readmission	Absence of documented discharge planning associated with adverse outcomes after discharge

▶

Table 10.1 continued

Source	Design & Sample	Intervention(s)	Conclusions
Hakim & Bakheit, 1998	Obs; n = 46 stroke patients	Analysis of the relative importance of factors on length of stay (LoS)	Delay in provision of equipment and home adaptations and placement in a nursing home were the best predictors of prolonged LoS

CCT   Controlled clinical trial
GP   General practitioner (family doctor)
LoS   Length of stay
Obs   Observational study
RCT   Randomised controlled trial
M/A   Meta-analysis (including systematic review)
Entries in italic denote studies that are not specific to stroke

Table 11.1 Late rehabilitation after stroke

Source	Design & Sample	Intervention(s)	Conclusions
Lehman et al, 1975	CCT; n = 114; patients late after stroke	Inpatient specialist multiprofessional input	Late rehabilitation reduced dependence in ADL; cost-effective
Tangeman et al, 1990	CCT; n = 40; patients over 1 year after stroke	Outpatient therapy; 2 hours/day, 4 days/week; 5 weeks	Reduced disability (ADL) and reduced impairment (balance performance)
Jongbloed & Morgan, 1991	RCT; n = 40; patients discharged from rehabilitation	Therapy for, or questions about, leisure from occupational therapy	No differences in leisure activity or satisfaction with activity
Wade et al, 1992	RCT; n = 92; patients with reduced mobility 2–6 years after stroke	Home-based assessment and treatment from experienced physiotherapist	Therapy improved mobility for 3+ months, but patients deteriorated when untreated
Dam et al, 1993	CCT; n = 51; patients 3 months after stroke	Outpatient rehabilitation for up to 2 years, on and off	Reduced disability after rehabilitation
Drummond & Walker, 1995	RCT; n = 65; patients six months after stroke	Occupational therapy, general or focused on leisure, or no therapy	Therapy focused on leisure improved leisure
Werner & Kessler, 1996	RCT*; n = 40; patients >1 year after stroke	Nothing, or 12 weeks of 4 days/week 2 hours/day therapy	Therapy reduced dependence and increased social function, and effect was maintained; control group deteriorated
Walker et al, 1996	RCT; n = 15; patients unable to dress 6 months post-stroke	Occupational therapy focused on dressing	Focused therapy improved independence in dressing
Baskett et al, 1999	RCT; n = 100 stroke patients discharged from hospital	Home visits by therapist once a week; prescribed programme of exercises compared with outpatient or day hospital therapy	No statistical differences between control and intervention group. A supervised home-based programme is as effective as outpatient or day hospital therapy

ADL   Activities of daily living
CCT   Controlled clinical trial
RCT   Randomised controlled trial (* = minor variation in design)

Table 11.2 Social support after discharge

Source	Design & Sample	Intervention(s)	Conclusions
Christie & Weigall, 1984	RCT; n = 213 patients late after stroke	Social worker visits 2 yr after stroke (7 in 12 months) to evaluate effect on patient activities and use of services	No difference in activities score (Katz Index) or number of days in hospital
Evans et al, 1988	RCT; n = 206 rehabilitation stroke patients	Nothing, education, or education and counselling sessions for carers soon after stroke.	Education and counselling resulted in better knowledge, more effective problem solving and adjustment at 12 months
Towle et al, 1989	RCT; n = 44 depressed stroke patients at home	Information ± additional social worker support	No difference in mood, equipment or services
Hansen, 1990	*RCT; n = 100 patients with neurological disease*	*Intensive social assistance at and after discharge*	*Many unmet needs at discharge. No differences in satisfaction, but readmission less, more problems solved*
Friedland & McColl, 1992	RCT; n = 88; stroke patients at home after rehabilitation	Special social support intervention, or nil (normal service)	No difference in social support or psychosocial function (GHQ, SIP)
Nouri & Lincoln, 1993	RCT; n = 52 stroke patients	Stroke drivers' screening assessment (SDSA) for intervention group compared with normal assessment by GP	SDSA predicted road performance in 81% of those tested; GP assessment correctly predicted 56%
Forster & Young, 1996	RCT; n = 240, patients at home after stroke	Specialist nurse visits (6+ over 6 months) or normal services alone	No beneficial effect on patient's disability, social activities, or mood; or carer's stress
Dennis et al, 1997	RCT; n = 417 patients 30 days post-stroke	Family care worker (FCW) or standard care	FCW group more satisfied; but possible increase in patient helplessness; no other differences detected

GHQ General health questionnaire
GP   General practitioner (family doctor)
RCT Randomised controlled trial
SIP   Sickness impact profile
Entries in italic denote studies that are not specific to stroke

Table 11.3 Secondary prevention after stroke

Source	Design & Sample	Intervention(s)	Conclusions
Antiplatelet Trialists Collaboration (APTC), 1994	M/A; n = 10,000 patients at risk of stroke or TIA	Prolonged antiplatelet therapy (75–325 mg aspirin) as prophylaxis for vascular events.	Overall one-third reduction in death, myocardial infarction and stroke
Koudstaal, 1995a	M/A; n = 1 trial, 455 patients	Warfarin (INR 2.5–4.0) or aspirin or placebo	Rate of recurrence reduced from 10% to 4% per year; and other vascular events reduced
Koudstaal, 1995b	M/A; n = 1 trial; 782 patients without AF or with contra-indications to anticoagulation	Aspirin (300 mg daily) or placebo	Insufficient data, but aspirin seems safe and to have some effect

▶

Table 11.3 continued

Source	Design & Sample	Intervention(s)	Conclusions
Hebert et al, 1997	S/R; 16 trials; n = 29,000	Statin drugs alone used to reduce lipid levels	Large reductions in cholesterol, and clear evidence of reduction in stroke risk and total CVD mortality
Cutler et al, 1997	S/R; 32 trials; n = 2635	Reducing dietary sodium	Effects on lowering blood pressure dependent on substantial lowering of dietary sodium
Midgley et al, 1996	M/A; 56 trials, n = 1131 hypertensive, 2374 normotensive subjects	Trials with randomised allocation to control and dietary sodium intervention groups and observation of BP	Decreases in BP larger in trials of older hypertensives, and non-significant in normotensives
Blauw et al, 1997	M/A; 13 trials; n = 20,438.	3-Hydroxy-3-methylglutaryl-coenzyme (HMG-CoA) reductase inhibitor vs randomised placebo controls	Combined data suggest HMG-CoA reductase inhibitors prevent stroke in middle age. Need for more trials to determine effect in the elderly
Crouse et al, 1997, 1998	M/A; 4 trials primary prevention; 8 trials secondary prevention of CHD	Reductase inhibitor monotherapy	Significant reduction in expected stroke incidence. Greater for secondary prevention group (32% reduction) than primary prevention (27%)
Kawachi et al, 1993	Obs; n = 117,006 women aged 30–55 years	To assess the relationship of time since stopping smoking to risk of stroke	The excess risk of stroke among former cigarette smokers largely disappeared 2–4 years after cessation
European Atrial Fibrillation Trial (EAFT), 1993	RCT; n = 1007 patients, non-rheumatic atrial fibrillation	Aspirin/placebo/warfarin (669) or aspirin/placebo (338)	For each 1000 patient-years, warfarin prevents 90 events and aspirin 40 events
European Atrial Fibrillation Trial (EAFT), 1995	Obs; n = 214 patients taking warfarin in RCT	INR and rate of stroke	Optimal INR 2.0–3.9; less gave no benefit, more associated with haemorrhage
Post-stroke Antihypertensive Treatment Study (PATS) Collaborative Group, 1995	RCT; n = 5665 patients with a history of stroke or TIA	Antihypertensive treatment for patients with history of stroke/TIA; 2 year follow-up	Blood pressure reduction by 5–2 mmHg reduced incidence of stroke by 29%
Wannamethee et al, 1995	Obs; n = 7735 men aged 40–59 years	To examine the effects of giving up smoking, years since cessation and quantity smoked	Smoking cessation is associated with a decreased risk. Complete loss of risk not seen in heavy smokers. Most benefit in hypertensive subjects
CAPRIE Steering Committee, 1996	RCT; n = 19,185 patients with cardiovascular disease (6431 with cerebrovascular disease)	Clopidogrel vs aspirin in patients at risk of ischaemic events	Clopidogrel is as effective and safe as medium-dose aspirin
Diener et al, 1996	RCT; n = 6602 patients with prior stroke or TIA	Aspirin, dipyridamole slow release, both and neither	A combination of aspirin and dipridamole may be more beneficial than either alone, and dipyridamole may be as effective as aspirin

Table 11.3 continued

Source	Design & Sample	Intervention(s)	Conclusions
Elliott et al 1996	Standardised cross sectional study within and across populations n = 10,074 men and women aged 20–59yrs	Assessment of daily urinary sodium excretion to blood pressure (BP) and age	Higher urinary sodium is associated with substantially greater differences (higher) systolic BP in middle age compared to young adulthood
Stroke Prevention in Reversible Ischaemia Trial (SPIRIT), 1997	RCT; n = 1243 patients with TIA or minor stroke	Aspirin vs anticoagulants (INR 3-4.4; ie higher than normally used in the UK)	Trial stopped owing to excess haemorrhage in the anticoagulant group.
Wannamethee et al, 1998	Obs; n = 7142 men aged 40–59 years	To examine the relationship between modifiable lifestyle factors (smoking, physical activity, alcohol intake, and BMI) and survival free of cardiovascular disease	Increased smoking and BMI levels were associated with myocardial infarction, stroke and diabetes. Moderate physical activity was associated with reduced risk
Lightowlers & McGuire, 1998	Cost-modelling data from RCTs	Warfarin for non-rheumatic atrial fibrillation; primary prevention	Cost of life-year free of stroke = −£400 to +£13,000; sensitive to cost of anti-coagulation monitoring services
Whelton et al, 1998	RCT; n = 975 men and women aged 60–80 with diagnosis of high blood pressure	585 obese: reduced dietary sodium, weight loss, both or usual care; 390 non-obese: reduced sodium or usual care	Reduced sodium intake and weight loss feasible, effective and safe as non-pharmacological therapy in older persons

AF	Atrial fibrillation
BMI	Body mass index
CHD	Coronary heart disease
CVD	Cardiovascular disease
INR	International normalised ratio
M/A	Meta-analysis
Obs	Observational study
RCT	Randomised controlled trial
S/R	Systematic review
TIA	Transient ischaemic attack

Table 11.4 Carotid surgery

Source	Design & Sample	Intervention(s)	Conclusions
Cina et al 1999	M/A; 2 trials, n = 5950 patients	Surgery for carotid stenosis compared to best medical treatment	Carotid endarterectomy reduced the risk of death or disabling stroke in surgically fit patients with measured 50% (NASCET) 70%(ECST) stenosis, by surgeons with low complication rates (<6%)
Young et al, 1996	Obs; n = 179 arteriograms (99 patients)	Interpretation (measurement) of three radiologists compared	Systematic variation and other variation observed; could affect decisions in 3–6% of patients
Moore et al, 1996	Obs; n = 5641 operations and 117 surgeons	Selection of surgeons by criteria; measurement of morbidity and mortality	Surgeons with 12+ operations per year; documentation of 50; and low complication rate retain low rate.

▶

Table 11.4 continued

Source	Design & Sample	Intervention(s)	Conclusions
Nussbaum et al, 1996	Obs; n = 150 patients with carotid endarterectomy	Calculation of cost-effectiveness using their data	Carotid endarterectomy is cost-effective if morbidity and mortality low
Kuntz & Kent, 1996	Model; RCT data	Calculations on cost per QALY from RCT data	Cost per QALY = $4,000–$50,000; depending on assumptions
Martin et al, 1997	Obs; n = 508 referrals with minor stroke or transient ischaemic attack for surgery	Agreed TIA/stroke in 373; but vascular area in only 315. No single alternative diagnosis stands out	Patients referred for carotid surgery need careful neurological evaluation first
McCollum et al, 1997	Obs; n = 709 patients and 59 surgeons	Carotid endarterectomy; outcome studied	Low risk of stroke/death (3%), but increased if operated on by trainee
European Carotid Surgery Trialists' Collaborative Group (ECST), 1998	RCT; n = 3024 patients; acute non-disabling acute cerebrovascular event	Carotid endarterectomy for carotid stenosis	Benefit (absolute 11%) if carotid stenosis on symptomatic side 80%–99%
North American Symptomatic Carotid Endarterectomy Trial Collaborators (NASCET 1998)	RCT; n = 2267 patients	Carotid endarterectomy for carotid stenosis	Clear benefit from surgery for those with stenoses of more than 70%

CEA   Carotid endarterectomy
Obs   Observational study
QALY Quality adjusted life year
RCT   Randomised controlled trial

Table 12.1 Accuracy of diagnosis and classification

Source	Design & Sample	Result(s)	Conclusions
Chambers et al, 1983	Obs; n = 700 stroke unit referrals	84 (12%) non-stroke: migraine (23), tumours (12), psychogenic (12)	Misdiagnosis occurs; review of clinical diagnosis is needed
Kraaijeveld et al, 1984	Clinical diagnosis of TIA by two neurologists	Agreed that 36 of 52 had and 12/52 had not had a TIA; disagreed on 8; kappa 0.65. Vascular area agreed 24/36	TIA is a poorly defined entity; agreement is low
Lindley et al, 1993	Two clinicians experienced in stroke examined and classified stroke; 85 patients	Agreed on sub-type in 56% (or 68% if best guess); kappa 0.41; reasonable to poor agreement on signs	Experienced clinicians agree more than chance, but not well; signs are often unreliably detected/recorded
Leibson et al, 1994	Hospital discharge ICD codes compared with prospective register	30 of 40 strokes occurring in hospital not recorded in hospital list; of 313 on register, only 239 had stroke as first diagnosis and 290 had stroke in first five diagnoses	Sensitivity and positive predictive value depend upon number of diagnoses considered, but data not very accurate
Toni et al, 1994	Early clinical diagnosis of lacunar stroke against final diagnosis	Of 219 initial diagnoses, 123 confirmed; of 170 finally diagnosed, 47 not diagnosed initially	Relevance to clinical practice uncertain

Table 12.1 continued

Source	Design & Sample	Result(s)	Conclusions
Madden et al, 1995	Prospective study; acute and three-month classification by neurologists compared	297/479 (62%) diagnoses unchanged at 3 months; 70 (15%) still unclassified at three months	Clinical classification using well defined criteria by well motivated experts not very consistent
Kothari et al, 1995a	Pre-hospital diagnosis by paramedics against final diagnosis (USA)	62 of 86 diagnoses correct; remainder had acute other illness	Relevant if hyperacute treatment becomes available
Kothari et al, 1995b	Diagnosis of admitting doctor compared with discharge diagnosis	Of 427 discharged, 422 correctly identified; of 441 admitted, 422 correct	Admitting doctor's diagnosis (with CT scan) usually correct (in USA)
Davenport et al, 1996a	Hospital discharge ICD codes compared with prospective register	Of 557 on hospital list, 529 had stroke (39 not on prospective register); 84 patients on register not on hospital list	Routine data not very reliable: sensitivity 529/613; positive predictive value 529/557
Benesch et al, 1997	Hospital discharge ICD codes compared with diagnosis after medical review of notes	ICD-9 codes 433–436 vary in accuracy between 77% and 85%	ICD classification accuracy very limited
Kothari et al, 1997	Items from National Institute of Health (in USA) stroke scale as diagnostic items	Three items (facial palsy, arm weakness, dysarthria) had sensitivity 100%, specificity 92%	Clinical features usually diagnostic of stroke could be used in emergency diagnosis
Mant et al, 1997	Hospital discharge ICD codes compared with prospective register	Of 318 on hospital list, 230 confirmed stroke (27 not on prospective register); 29 patients on register not on hospital list	Routine data not very reliable: sensitivity 230/263; positive predictive value 230/318
Martin et al, 1997	Obs; n = 508 referrals with minor stroke or TIA, for surgery	Agreed TIA/stroke in 37, but vascular area in only 315. No single alternative diagnosis stands out	Patients referred for carotid surgery need careful neurological evaluation first
Ferro et al, 1998	General practitioner and admitting doctor stroke diagnoses compared with neurologist's	44/52 GP diagnoses correct; 169/185 admitting doctor diagnoses confirmed	Routine clinical diagnosis is robust; absent or unusual history increases error
Goldstein 1998	Hospital discharge ICD-9-CM codes compared with medical review of discharge summary	ICD-9 codes 433, 434 and 436 are inaccurate in 15%–20% of cases; modifier codes did not help	Routine ICD classification remains unreliable
Stineman & Granger, 1998	FIM-FRGs compared with outcome and length of stay length of stay	21 groups of patients identified; close relationship to length of stay, but vary	Need large number of groups to capture variation among patients

CT   Computed tomograhy
FIM-FRG Functional independence measure – function related group
GP   General Practitioner (family doctor)
ICD   International classification of disease
ICD-9-CM International classification of disease (version 9, Clinically Modified)
TIA   Transient ischaemic attack

Table 12.2 Outcome measures

Source	Design & Sample	Measure(s) & Analysis	Conclusions
Stolee et al, 1992	Obs; n = 15 elderly patients in 2 geriatric services	Goal attainment score (GAS) follow-up guides scored independently by 2 geriatricians	GAS feasible as a method of outcome evaluation in geriatric care settings
Rockwood et al, 1993, 1997	Obs; n = 45 frail elderly; n = 44 cognitive rehabilitation patients	A range of standardised outcome measures compared with GAS	GAS proved more responsive to change than any other measure (Does not study effect of goal setting itself)
Harwood et al, 1994	Obs; n = 141 patients at home 6 months post-stroke	London handicap scale and others; correlations and variance	London handicap scale is valid and reliable as a postal questionnaire
Lindley et al, 1994	RCT; 60 patients, 6–9 months post-stroke	Postal or telephone questionnaires: complex and simple	Confirmed utility of two simple outcome questions
Duncan et al, 1995	Obs; n = 58 stroke patients pre-and 68 post-opening of a stroke unit	Evaluation of management and outcomes using specific indicators based on agreed issues	Reduction in mortality from 37.9% to 22%; improvements on all measures
Visser et al, 1995	16 randomly selected stroke patients 6+ months post-stroke	HAD, NHP, SIP; time taken; test-retest; detecting differences	All three feasible, and equal on most aspects
Wellwood et al, 1995	159 one-year survivors	OPCS and Barthel ADL index compared	Closely correlated (r = −0.73) but OPCS useful at ceiling and floor of Barthel
Anderson et al, 1996	90 patients at home one year after stroke	SF-36, GHQ-28, AAP, Barthel	SF-36 valid for physical and mental health, but not good for social functioning
Elmstahl et al, 1996	n = 150 patients with stroke or dementia	Caregiver burden scale (22 items, five factors)	Scale is valid and reliable assessment of burden
Scholte op Reimer et al, 1996	n = 327 patients 6 months after stroke	Patient satisfaction with services	Dissatisfaction associated with perceived unmet care needs and with emotional distress, not with continuity of care
Sneeuw et al, 1997	437 patients, six months post-stroke	SIP; comparison of proxy and patient	Proxy-obtained data have some bias, but worth collecting if patient incompetent
Dorman et al, 1997	152 patients at home 43–107 weeks post-stroke	EuroQol, Barthel, HAD, FAI, OPCS, pain VAS	EuroQol has concurrent and discriminatory validity by interview and/or self completion
Mathias et al, 1997	33 patients, and their carers, stroke in last 3 months	HUI; interviewer asked patient and carer separately	Caregivers gave similar answers; proxy assessment reasonable
Duncan et al, 1997	Obs; n = 304 people with 'mild' stroke: 184 after TIA and 654 'normals'	Barthel ADL index, SF-36, depression	SF-36 sensitive to differences while Barthel at ceiling; depression associated with dependence
O'Rourke et al, 1998	105 patients, six months post-stroke; comparison	GHQ, HAD, formal psychiatric assessment; ROC	GHQ and HAD equivalent; cut-off used depends upon desired sensitivity/ specificity
Dorman et al, 1998	443 patients, six months post-stroke; comparison	EuroQol, SF-36; reliability	Reliability similar, but considerable variance

Table 12.2 continued

Source	Design & Sample	Measure(s) & Analysis	Conclusions
O'Mahony et al, 1998	104 patients at home after stroke	SF-36 posted to patients; completion rates in total and for items	83% response, but many items not complete; not suitable as routine measure
Scholte op Reimer et al, 1998a, b	Obs; n = 166 and 47; carers 6 months and 17 months post-stroke	Study of validity and reliability of SCQ	SCQ (27 questions) can assess burden of care-giving
Dorman et al, 1999	Obs; n = 688 patients late after stroke, at home	Comparison of EuroQol and SF-36	Reasonable cross-correlation, except on mental health domain
Pound et al, 1999	Obs; n = 274 patients, 4 and 12 months post-stroke	Relationship between patient satisfaction and service provision and other outcomes	Greater satisfaction associated with greater service delivery and better outcome

AAP	Adelaide activities profile (derived from FAI)	OPCS	Office of population censuses and surveys disability scales
ADL	Activities of daily living	RCT	Randomised controlled trial
FAI	Frenchay activities index	ROC	Receiver operator curve
GAS	Goal attainment scaling	SCQ	Sense of competence questionnaire
GHQ	General health questionnaire	SF-36	Short form 36
HAD	Hospital anxiety and depression scale	SIP	Sickness impact profile (also known as functional limitation profile)
HUI	Health utilities index	TIA	Transient ischaemic attack
NHP	Nottingham health profile	VAS	Visual analogue scale
Obs	Observational study		

Entries in italic denote studies that are not specific to stroke

Table 12.3 Service audit/evaluation/comparison

Source	Design & Sample	Intervention(s)	Conclusions
Jessee & Schranz, 1990	Obs; n = 52 stroke patients (and 118 others)	Relationship between mortality rate and quality of care independently assessed	No relationship detected between mortality rate and quality of care
Shah et al, 1990	Obs; n = 258 first stroke patients	Multivariate investigation of factors affecting outcome (length of stay, disability)	Only 17–30% of variance explained by wide range of patient factors, including social factors
Gompertz et al, 1995	CCT; n = 261 acute strokes; two adjacent health districts	One had comprehensive stroke service with stroke unit, the other did not. But many other differences between districts	No observed difference in process or outcome; effect of stroke service will depend upon context
Mant & Hicks, 1995	*Theoretical analysis of myocardial infarction*	*Likelihood of outcome or process measure detecting real difference*	*Process measure much more efficient at detecting real difference*
McNaughton, 1996	Obs; n = 50, case notes	District hospital, no stroke unit	RCP package easy to use and relevant
Davenport et al, 1996b	Obs; 468 patients: 216 before stroke service, 252 in stroke service	Investigated 30 day case fatality, living at home, and independence	Apparent 'improvements' after stroke service lost once adjusted for case-mix
Lee et al, 1997	Random sample of Medicare stroke patients; n = 25,624 patients	Studied patient variables, market variables and resource use	Patient variables account for less than 30% of variance; most variance unexplained
Poloniecki, 1998	*Statistical arguments*	*Theoretical audit of operative complications*	*Local (in-house) systems may be better*
Marshall & Spiegelhalter, 1998	*Data-driven analysis of outcome of health intervention*	*Analysis of league tables of in vitro fertilisation*	*Sampling variability dominates rank and change in rank*
Poloniecki et al, 1998	*Data-driven analysis of outcome of health intervention*	*Analysis of league tables of mortality from heart surgery*	*Sampling variability dominates rank and change in rank*

CCT   Controlled clinical trial
Obs   observational study
RCP   Royal College of Physicians (stroke audit package)
Entries in italic denote studies that are not specific to stroke

References

Ada L, Vattanasilp W, O'Dwyer NJ, Crosbie J (1998) Does spasticity contribute to walking dysfunction after stroke? *Journal of Neurology, Neurosurgery and Psychiatry* **64**: 628–35.

Agency for Health Care Policy and Research (1995) Post-stroke rehabilitation – Clinical Practice Guideline No 16. USA:AHCPR.

Allman P, Hope T, Fairburn CG (1992) Crying following stroke: a report of 30 cases. *General Hospital Psychiatry* **14**: 315–24.

Ancliffe J (1992)Strapping the shoulder in patients following a cerebrovascular accident (CVA): a pilot study. Australian Journal of Physiotherapy **38**: 37–41.

Andersen G, Vestergaard K, Rils JO (1993) Citalopram for post-stroke pathological crying. Lancet **342**: 837–39.

Andersen G, Vestergaard K, Lauritsen L (1994) Effective treatment of post-stroke depression with the selective serotonin re-uptake inhibitor citalopram. *Stroke* **25**: 1099–104.

Anderson R (1992) The aftermath of stroke: the experience of patients and their families. Cambridge University Press.

Anderson CS, Linto J, Stewart-Wynne EG (1995) A population-based assessment of the impact and burden of caregiving for long-term stroke survivors. *Stroke*; **26**: 843–9

Anderson C, Laubscher S, Burns R (1996) Validation of the Short Form 36 (SF-36) health survey questionnaire among stroke patients. *Stroke*; **27**: 1812–6

Antiplatelet Trialists Collaboration (APTC) (1994) Collaborative overview of randomised trials of antiplatelet therapy. *British Medical Journal* **308**: 81–106.

a'Rogvi-Hansen B, Boysen G (1994) Glycerol treatment in acute ischaemic stroke (Cochrane Review). In: The Cochrane Library, Issue 3, 1999. Oxford: Update Software.

Association of Chartered Physiotherapists with special Interest in Neurology (ACPIN) (1995) Recommendations for physiotherapy practice and service development in neurology

Astrom G (1996) Generalised anxiety disorder in stroke patients: a 3 year longitudinal study. *Stroke* **27**: 270–5.

Axelsson R, Asplund K, Norberg A, Alafuzoff I (1988) Nutritional status in patients with acute stroke. *Acta Medica Scandinavia*; **224**: 217–24.

Bar-Eli M, Hartman I, Levy-Kolker N (1994) Using goal setting to improve physical performance of adolescents with behaviour disorders: the effects of goal proximity. *Adapted Physical Activity Quarterly* **11**: 86–97.

Bar-Eli M, Tenenbaum G, Pie JS, *et al*, (1997) Effect of goal difficulty, goal specificity and duration of practice time intervals on muscular endurance performance. *Journal of Sports Sciences* **15**: 125–35.

Baskett JJ, Broad JB, Reekie G, *et al*, (1999) Shared responsibility for ongoing rehabilitation: a new approach to home-based therapy after stroke. *Clinical Rehabilitation* **13**: 23–33.

Basmajian JV, Kulkulka CG, Narayan MG, Takebe K (1975) Biofeedback treatment of foot-drop after stroke compared with standard rehabilitation technique: effects on voluntary control and strength. *Archives of Physical Medicine and Rehabilitation* **56**: 231–6.

Basmajian JV, Gowland CA, Brandstater ME, *et al*, (1982) EMG feedback treatment of upper limb in hemiplegic stroke patients: a pilot study. *Archives of Physical Medicine and Rehabilitation* **63**: 613–6.

Basmajian JV, Gowland CA, Finlayson MA, *et al*, (1987) Stroke treatment: comparison of integrated behavioural-physical therapy vs traditional physical therapy programs. *Archives of Physical Medicine and Rehabilitation* **68**: 267–72.

Bath P, Bath F (1996) Prostacyclin and analogues for acute ischaemic stroke (Cochrane Review). In: The Cochrane Library, Issue 3, 1999. Oxford: Update Software.

Bath PMW, Bath FJ, Asplund K (1996). Pentoxifylline, propentofylline and pentifylline for acute ischaemic stroke (Cochrane Review). In: The Cochrane Library, Issue 3, 1999. Oxford: Update Software.

Beckerman H, Becher J, Lankhorst GJ, *et al*, (1996a) The efficacy of thermo-coagulation of the tibial nerve and a polypropylene ankle-foot orthosis on spasticity of the leg in stroke patients: results of a randomised clinical trial. *Clinical Rehabilitation* **10**: 112–20.

Beckerman H, Becher J, Lankhorst GJ, Verbeek ALM (1996b) Walking ability of stroke patients: efficacy of thermocoagulation of tibial nerve blocking and a polypropylene ankle-foot orthosis. *Archives of Physical Medicine and Rehabilitation* **77**: 1144–51.

Beech R, Rudd AG, Tilling K, Wolfe CDA (1999) Economic consequences of early inpatient discharge to community based rehabilitation for stroke in an inner-London teaching hospital. *Stroke* **30**: 729–35.

Benesch C, Witter DM, Wilder AL, *et al*, (1997) Inaccuracy of the International Classification of Disease (ICD-9-CM) in identifying the diagnosis of ischaemic cerebrovascular disease. *Neurology* **49**: 660–4.

Bereczki D, Fekete I (1997) Vinpocetine for acute ischaemic stroke (Cochrane Review). In: The Cochrane Library, Issue 3, 1999. Oxford: Update Software.

Berry MW, Rinke WJ, Smicklas-Wright H (1989) Work-site health promotion: the effects of a goal-setting program on nutrition-related behaviours. *Journal of the American Dietetic Association* **89**: 914–20.

Bertakis KD (1991) Impact of a patient education intervention on appropriate utilisation of clinic services. *Journal of the American Board of Family Practitioners* **4**: 411–8.

Bhakta BB, Cozens JA, Bamford JM, Chamberlain MA (1996) Use of botulinum toxin in stroke patients with severe upper limb spasticity. *Journal of Neurology, Neurosurgery and Psychiatry* **61**: 30–5.

Blair CE (1995) Combining behaviour management and mutual goal setting to reduce physical dependency in nursing home residents. *Nursing Research* **44**: 160–5.

Blair CE, Lewis R, Vieweg V, Tucker R (1996) Group and single-subject evaluation of a programme to promote self-care in elderly nursing home residents. *Journal of Advanced Nursing* **24**: 1207–13.

Blauw GJ, Lagaay AM, Smelt AH, Westendorp RG (1997) Stroke, statins and cholesterol. A meta-analysis of randomised, placebo-controlled, double blind trials with HMG-CoA reductase inhibitors. *Stroke* **28**: 946–50.

Blood Pressure in Acute Stroke Collaboration (BASC) (1997) Blood pressure management in acute stroke. Part 1. Assessment of trials designed to alter blood pressure (Cochrane Review). In: The Cochrane Library, Issue 1, 1999. Oxford. Update Software.

Borello-France DF, Burdett RG, Gee ZL (1988) Modification of sitting posture of patients with hemiplegia using seat boards and backboards. *Physical Therapy* **68**: 67–71.

Bots ML, van der Wilk EC, Koudstaal PJ, *et al*, (1997) Transient neurological attacks in the general population. Prevalence, risk factors, and clinical relevance. *Stroke* **28**: 768–73.

Bowen J, Yaste C (1994) Effect of a stroke protocol on hospital costs of stroke patients. *Neurology* **44**: 1961–4.

Bowman BR, Baker LL, Waters RL (1979) Positional feedback and electrical stimulation: an automated treatment for the hemiplegic wrist. *Archives of Physical Medicine and Rehabilitation* **60**: 497–502.

Bradley L, Hart BB, Mandana S, *et al*, (1998) Electromyographic biofeedback for gait training after stroke. *Clinical Rehabilitation* **12**: 11–22.

Braus DF, Kraus JK, Strobel J (1994) The shoulder-hand syndrome after stroke: a prospective clinical trial. *Annals of Neurology* **36**: 728–33.

Brindley P, Copeland M, Demain C, Martyn P (1989) A comparison of the speech of ten chronic Broca's aphasics following intensive and non-intensive periods of therapy. *Aphasiology* **3**: 695–707.

Brown DA, Kautz SA (1998) Increased workload enhances force output during pedalling exercise in persons with post-stroke hemiplegia. *Stroke* **29**: 598–606.

Brown KW, Sloan RL, Pentland B (1998) Fluoxetine as a treatment for post-stroke emotionalism. *Acta Psychiatrica Scandinavia* **98**: 455–8.

Bruce C, Howard D (1987) Computer-generated phonemic cues: an effective aid for naming in aphasia. *British Journal of Disorders of Communication* **22**: 191–201.

Burbaud P, Wiart L, Dubos JL, *et al*, (1996) A randomised, double-blind, placebo-controlled trial of botulinum toxin in the treatment of spastic foot in hemiparetic patients. *Journal of Neurology, Neurosurgery and Psychiatry* 61: 265–9.

Burnside IG, Tobias HS, Bursill D (1982) Electromyographic feedback in the remobilisation of stroke patients: a controlled trial. *Archives of Physical Medicine and Rehabilitation* **63**: 217–22.

Burridge JH, Taylor PN, Hagan SA, *et al*, (1997) The effects of common peroneal stimulation on the effort and speed of walking: a randomised controlled trial with chronic hemiplegic patients. *Clinical Rehabilitation* **11**: 201–10.

Burt AA, Currie S (1978) A double-blind controlled trial of baclofen and diazepam in spasticity due to cerebrovascular lesions. In: Jukes AM (Ed) Baclofen: spasticity and cerebral pathology. Cambridge Medical Publications: 77–9.

Bynum HS, Rogers JC (1987) The use and effectiveness of assistive devices possessed by patients seen in home care. *Occupational Therapy Journal of Research* **7**: 181–91.

Campion E, Jette A, Berkman B (1983) An interdisciplinary geriatric consultation service: a controlled trial. *Journal of the American Geriatric Society* **31**: 792–6.

Candelise L, Ciccone A (1999) Gangliosides for acute ischaemic stroke (Cochrane Review). In: The Cochrane Library, Issue 3, 1999. Oxford. Update Software.

CAPRIE Steering Committee (1996) A randomised, blinded, trial of clopidogrel versus aspirin in patients at risk of ischaemic events (CAPRIE). *Lancet* **348**: 1329–39.

Carey JR (1990) Manual stretch: effect on finger movement control and force control in stroke patients with spastic extrinsic finger flexor muscles. *Archives of Physical Medicine and Rehabilitation* **71**: 888–94.

Carr EK, Kenney FD (1992) Positioning of the stroke patient: a review of the literature. *International Journal of Nursing Studies* **29**: 355–69.

Chae J, Bethoux F, Bohine T, *et al*, (1998) Neuromuscular stimulation for upper extremity motor and functional recovery in acute hemiplegia. *Stroke* **29**: 975–9.

Chamberlain MA, Thornley G, Stowe J, Wright V (1981) Evaluation of aids and equipment for the bath. II Possible solutions to the problem. *Rheumatology and Rehabilitation* **20**: 38–43.

Chambers BR, Donnan GA, Bladin PF (1983) Patterns of stroke. An analysis of the first 700 consecutive admissions to the Austin hospital stroke unit. *Australian and New Zealand Journal of Medicine* **13**: 57–64.

Chantraine A, Baribeault A, Uebelhart D, Gremion G (1999) Shoulder pain and dysfunction in hemiplegia: effects of functional electrical stimulation. *Archives of Physical Medicine and Rehabilitation* **3**: 328–31.

Charles C, Gauld M, Chambers L, *et al*, (1994) How was your hospital stay? Patients' reports about their care in Canadian hospitals. *Canadian Medical Association Journal* **150**: 1813–22.

Chartered Society of Physiotherapy, College of Occupational Therapy and Royal College of Nursing (1997) Joint statement: Physiotherapy Frontline Sept 3; document PA41. London: Chartered Society of Physiotherapy.

Childers MK, Stacy M, Cooke DL, Stonnington HH (1996) Comparison of two injection techniques using botulinum toxin in spastic hemiplegia. *American Journal of Physical Medicine and Rehabilitation* **75**: 462–9.

Chinese Acute Stroke Trial collaborative group. CAST 1997. Randomised, placebo-controlled trial of early aspirin use in 20,000 patients with acute ischaemic stroke. *Lancet* **349**: 1641–9.

Christie D, Weigall D (1984) Social work effectiveness in two-year stroke survivors: a randomised controlled trial. *Community Health Studies* **8**: 26–32.

Cina CS, Clase CM, Haynes RB (1999) Carotid endarterectomy for symptomatic carotid stenosis (Cochrane Review). In: The Cochrane Library, Issue 3, 1999. Oxford: Update Software.

Clark MS, Smith DS (1998) Factors contributing to patient satisfaction with rehabilitation following stroke. *International Journal of Rehabilitation Research* **21**: 143–54.

Clinical Standards Advisory Group (1998) Report on clinical effectiveness using stroke care as an example. London: Stationery Office.

Coast J, Richards SH, Peters TJ, *et al*, (1998) Hospital at home or acute hospital care? A cost minimisation analysis. *British Medical Journal* **316**: 1802–6.

Colborne GR, Olney SJ, Griffin MP (1993) Feedback of ankle joint angle and soleus electromyography in the rehabilitation of hemiplegic gait. *Archives of Physical Medicine and Rehabilitation* **74**: 1100–6.

Corcoran PJ, Jebsen RH, Brengelmann GL, Simons BC (1970) Effects of plastic and metal leg braces on speed and energy cost of hemiparetic ambulation. *Archives of Physical Medicine and Rehabilitation* **51**: 69–77.

Corr S, Bayer A (1995) Occupational therapy for stroke patients after hospital discharge; a randomised controlled trial. *Clinical Rehabilitation* **9**: 291–6.

Corry IS, Cosgrove AP, Walsh EG, *et al*, (1997) Botulinum toxin A in the hemiplegic upper limb: a double-blind trial. *Developmental Medicine and Child Neurology* **39**: 185–93.

Corry IS, Cosgrove AP, Duffy CM, *et al*, (1998) Botulinum toxin A compared with stretching casts in the treatment of spastic equinus: a randomised prospective trial. *Journal of Paediatric Orthopaedics* **18**: 304–11.

Counsell C, Sandercock P (1998) Antiplatelet therapy for acute ischaemic stroke (Cochrane Review). In: The Cochrane Library, Issue 3, 1999. Oxford. Update Software.

Counsell C, Sandercock P (1999) Low-molecular-weight heparins or heparinoids versus standard unfractionated heparin for acute ischaemic stroke (Cochrane Review). In: The Cochrane Library, Issue 3, 1999. Oxford: Update Software.

Cozean CD, Pease WS, Hubbell SL (1988) Biofeedback and functional electrical stimulation in stroke rehabilitation. *Archives of Physical Medicine and Rehabilitation* **69**: 401–5.

Crisostomo EA, Duncan PW, Propst M, *et al*, (1988) Evidence that amphetamine with physical therapy promotes recovery of motor function in stroke patients. *Annals of Neurology* **23**: 94–7.

Crouse JR 3rd, Byington RP, Hoen HM, Furberg CD (1997) Reductase inhibitor monotherapy and stroke prevention. *Archives of Internal Medicine* **157**: 1305–10.

Crouse JR 3rd, Byington RP, Furberg CD (1998) HMG-CoA reductase inhibitor therapy and stroke risk reduction: an analysis of clinical trials data. *Atherosclerosis* 138 **1**: 11–24.

Crow JL, Lincoln NB, Nouri FM, De Weerdt W (1989) The effectiveness of EMG biofeedback in the treatment of arm function after stroke. *International Disability Studies* **11**: 155–60.

Cummings V, Kerner JF, Arones S, Steinbock C (1985) Day hospital service in rehabilitation medicine: an evaluation. *Archives of Physical Medicine and Rehabilitation* **66**: 86–91.

Cunningham C, Horgan F, Keane N, *et al*, (1996) Detection of disability by different members of an interdisciplinary team. *Clinical Rehabilitation* **10**: 247–54.

Cutler JA, Follmann D, Allender PS (1997) Randomised trials of sodium reduction: an overview. *American Journal of Clinical Nutrition* 65(SupplS): 643S–651S.

Dam M, Tonin P, Casson S, *et al*, (1993) The effects of long-term rehabilitation therapy on post-stroke hemiplegic patients. *Stroke* **24**: 1186–91.

Dam M, Tonin P, De Boni A, *et al*, (1996) Effects of fluoxetine and maprotiline on functional recovery in post-stroke hemiplegic patients undergoing rehabilitation therapy. *Stroke* **27**: 1211–14.

Daniels SK, Brailey K, Priestly DH, *et al*, (1998) Aspiration in patients with acute stroke. *Archives of Physical Medicine and Rehabilitation* 79: 14–9.

Davalos A, Ricart W, Gonzalez-Huix F, *et al*, (1996) Effect of early malnutrition after acute stroke on clinical outcome. *Stroke* **27**: 1028–32.

Davenport RJ, Dennis MS, Warlow CP (1996a) The accuracy of Scottish Morbidity Record (SMR1) data for identifying hospitalised stroke patients. *Health Bulletin* **54**: 402–5.

Davenport RJ, Dennis MS, Warlow CP (1996b) Effect of correcting outcome data for case mix: an example from stroke medicine. *British Medical Journal* **312**: 1503–5.

David R, Enderby P, Baniton D (1982) Treatment of acquired aphasia: speech therapists and volunteers compared. *Journal of Neurology, Neurosurgery and Psychiatry* **45**: 957–61.

Dean CM, Shepherd RB (1997) Task-related training improves performance of seating reaching tasks after stroke: a randomised controlled trial. *Stroke* **28**: 722–8.

Dekker JHM, Wagenaar RC, Lankhorst GJ, de Jong BA (1997) The painful hemiplegic shoulder: effects of intra-articular triamcinolone acetonide. *American Journal of Physical Medicine and Rehabilitation* **76**: 43–8.

Dekker R, Drost EAM, Groothof JW, *et al*, (1998) Effects of day-hospital rehabilitation in stroke patients: a review of randomised clinical trials. *Scandinavian Journal of Rehabilitation Medicine* **30**: 87–94.

Dennis M, O'Rourke S, Slattery J, *et al*, (1997) Evaluation of a stroke family care worker: results of a randomised controlled trial. *British Medical Journal* **314**: 1071–6.

Dennis M, O'Rourke S, Lewis S, *et al*, (1998) A quantitative study of the emotional outcome of people caring for stroke survivors. *Stroke* **29**: 1867–72.

DePippo KL, Holas MA, Reding MJ (1992) Validation of the 3-oz water swallow test for aspiration following stroke. *Archives of Neurology* **49**: 1259–61.

DePippo KL, Holas MA, Reding MJ, *et al*, (1994) Dysphagia therapy following stroke: a controlled trial. *Neurology* 1994 **44**: 1655–60.

Dickstein R, Hocherman S, Pillar T, Shaham R (1986) Stroke rehabilitation: three exercise therapy approaches. *Physical Therapy* **66**: 1233–8.

Diener H, Cinha L, Forbes C, *et al*, (1996) European Stroke Prevention Study 2 (ESPS2) Dipyridamole and acetylsalicylic acid in the secondary prevention of stroke. *Journal of the Neurological Sciences* **143**: 1–13.

Dorman PJ, Waddell F, Slattery J, *et al*, (1997) Is the EuroQol a valid measure of health-related quality of life after stroke? *Stroke* **28**: 1876–82.

Dorman P, Slattery J, Farrell B, *et al*, for the United Kingdom Collaborators in the International Stroke Trial (IST) (1998) Qualitative comparison of the reliability of health status assessments with the EuroQol and SF-36 questionnaires after stroke. *Stroke* **29**: 63–8.

Dorman PJ, Dennis M, Sandercock P, on behalf of the United Kingdom Collaborators in the International Stroke Trial (IST) (1999) How do scores on the EuroQol relate to scores on the SF36 after stroke? *Stroke* **30**: 2146–51.

Draper BM, Poulos CJ, Cole AM, *et al*, (1992) A comparison of caregivers for elderly stroke and dementia victims. Journal of the American Geriatrics Society 40: 896–901.

Drummond AER, Walker MF (1995) A randomised controlled trial of leisure rehabilitation after stroke. *Clinical Rehabilitation* **9**: 283–90.

Duncan G, Ritchie LC, Jamieson DM, McLean MA (1995) Acute stroke in South Ayrshire: comparative study of pre and post stroke units. *Health Bulletin* **53**: 159–66.

Duncan PW, Samsa GP, Weinberger M, *et al*, (1997) Health status in individuals with mild stroke. *Stroke* **28**: 740–5

Duncan P, Richards L, Wallace D, *et al*, (1998) A randomised controlled pilot study of a home-based exercise program for individuals with mild and moderate stroke. *Stroke* **29**: 2055–60.

Dursun E, Hamamci N, Donmez S, *et al*, (1996) Angular biofeedback device for sitting balance of stroke. *Stroke* **26**: 1354–7.

Eagle DJ, Guyatt GH, Patterson C, *et al*, (1991) Effectiveness of a geriatric day hospital. *Canadian Medical Association Journa*l **144**: 699–704.

Early Supported Discharge Trialists (1999). Services for reducing duration of hospital care for acute stroke patients (Cochrane Review). In: The Cochrane Library, Issue 3, 1999. Oxford: Update Software.

Ebrahim S, Barer D, Nouri F (1987) An audit of follow-up services for stroke patients after discharge from hospital. *International Disability Studies* **9**: 103–5.

Elliott P, Stamler J, Nichols R, *et al*, (Intersalt Co-operative Research Group) (1996) Intersalt revisited: further analyses of 24 hour sodium excretion and blood pressure within and across populations. *British Medical Journal* **312**: 1249–53.

Elmstahl S, Malmberg B, Annerstedt L (1996) Caregiver's burden of patients 3 years after stroke assessed by a novel caregiver burden scale. *Archives of Physical Medicine and Rehabilitation* **77**: 177–82.

Enderby P, Broeckx J, Hospers W, *et al*, (1994) Effect of piracetam on recovery and rehabilitation after stroke: a double-blind, placebo-controlled study. *Clinical Neuropharmacology* **17**: 320–31.

Enderby P, van de Gaag A, Reid D (1998) Clinical guidelines for speech & language therapy. London: Royal College of Speech and Language Therapists.

European Atrial Fibrillation Trial (EAFT) Study Group (1993) Secondary prevention in non-rheumatic atrial fibrillation after transient ischaemic attack or minor stroke. *Lancet,* **342**: 1255–1262

European Atrial Fibrillation Trial (EAFT) Study Group (1995) Optimal oral anticoagulation therapy in patients with nonrheumatic atrial fibrillation and recent cerebral ischemia. *New England Journal of Medicine* **333**: 5–10.

European Carotid Surgery Trialists' (ECST) Collaborative Group (1998) Randomised trial of endarterectomy for recently symptomatic carotid stenosis: final results of the MRC European carotid surgery trial (ECST). *Lancet* **351**: 1379–87.

Evans RL, Hendricks RD (1993) Evaluating hospital discharge planning: a randomised clinical trial. *Medical Care* **31**: 358–70.

Evans RL, Matlock A-L, Bishop DS, *et al*, (1988) Family intervention after stroke: does counselling or education help? *Stroke* **19**: 1243–9.

Faghri PD, Rodgers MM (1997) The effects of functional neuromuscular stimulation-augmented physical therapy in the functional recovery of hemiplegic arm in stroke patients. *Clinical Kinesiology* **51**: 9–15.

Faghri PD, Rodgers MM, Glaser RM, *et al*, (1994) The effects of functional electrical stimulation on shoulder subluxation, arm function recovery, and shoulder pain in hemiplegic stroke patients. *Archives of Physical Medicine and Rehabilitation* **75**: 73–9.

Fanthome Y, Lincoln NB, Drummond A, Walker MF (1995) The treatment of visual neglect using feedback of eye movements: a pilot study. *Disability and Rehabilitation* **17**: 413–17.

Ferro JM, Pinto AN, Falcao I, *et al*, (1998) Diagnosis of stroke by the non-neurologist: a validation study. *Stroke*: **29**: 1106–9.

Feys HM, De Weerdt WJ, Selz BE, *et al*, (1998) Effect of a therapeutic intervention for the hemiplegic upper limb in the acute phase after stroke: a single blind, randomised, controlled multi-centre trial. *Stroke* **29**: 785–92.

Finestone HM, Greene-Finestone LS, Wilson ES, Teasell RW (1995) Malnutrition in stroke patients in the rehabilitation service and at follow up: prevalence and predictors. *Archives of Physical Medicine & Rehabilitation* **76**: 310–6.

Flaherty JH, Miller DK, Coe RM (1992) Impact on caregivers of supporting urinary function in non-institutionalised, chronically ill seniors. *Gerontologist* **32**: 541–5.

Forster A, Young J (1996) Specialist nurse support for patients with stroke in the community: a randomised controlled trial. *British Medical Journal* **312**: 1642–6.

Forster A, Dowswell G, Young J, *et al*, (1999a) Effect of a physiotherapist-led stroke training programme on attitudes of nurses caring for patients after stroke. *Stroke* 13 **2**: 113–22.

Forster A, Young J, Langhorne P (1999b) Systematic review of day hospital care for elderly people: the Day Hospital Group. *British Medical Journal* **318**: 837–41.

Fredman L, Daly MP (1997) Weight change: an indicator of caregiver stress. *Journal of Aging and Health* **9**: 43–69.

Friedland JF, McColl M (1992) Social support intervention after stroke: results of a randomised trial. *Archives of Physical Medicine and Rehabilitation* **73**: 573–81.

Gardner L, Powell L, Page M (1993) An appraisal of a selection of products currently available to older consumers. *Applied Ergonomics* **24**: 35–9.

Gariballa SE, Parker SG, Taub N, Castleden M (1998) Nutritional status of hospitalised acute stroke patients. *British Journal of Nutrition* **79**: 481–7.

Garon BR, Engle M, Ormiston C (1997) A randomised control study to determine the effects of unlimited oral intake of water in patients with identified aspiration. *Journal of Neurologic Rehabilitation* **11**: 139–48.

Gelber DA, Good DC, Laven LJ, Verhulst SJ (1993) Causes of urinary incontinence after acute hemispheric stroke. *Stroke* **24** 3: 378–82.

George J, Binns VE, Clayden AD, Mulley GP (1988) Aids and adaptations for the elderly at home: underprovided, under-used and under-maintained. *British Medical Journal* **296**: 1365–6.

Gitlin LN, Levine R, Geiger C (1993) Adaptive device use by older adults with mixed disabilities. *Archives of Physical Medicine and Rehabilitation* **74**: 149–52.

Gitlin LN, Schemm RL, Landsberg L, Burgh D (1996) Factors predicting assistive device use in home by older people following rehabilitation. *Journal of Aging and Health* **8**: 554–75.

Gitlin LN, Luborsky MR, Schemm RL (1998) Emerging concerns of older stroke patients about assistive device use. *Gerontologist* **38**: 169–80.

Gladman JRF, Lincoln NB, Barer DH (1993) A randomised controlled trial of domiciliary and hospital-based rehabilitation for stroke patients after discharge from hospital. *Journal of Neurology, Neurosurgery and Psychiatry* 56: 960–6.

Gladman JRF, Lincoln NB (1994) Follow-up of a controlled trial of domiciliary stroke rehabilitation (Domino study). *Age and Ageing* 23: 9–13.

Gladman JRF, Whynes D, Lincoln NB (1994) Cost-comparison of domiciliary and hospital-based stroke rehabilitation. *Age and Ageing* 23: 241–5.

Gladman JRF, Juby LC, Clarke PA, *et al*, (1995) Survey of a domiciliary stroke rehabilitation service. *Clinical Rehabilitation* 9: 245–9.

Glanz M, Klawansky S, Stason W, *et al*, (1995) Biofeedback therapy in post-stroke rehabilitation: a meta-analysis of the randomised controlled trials. *Archives of Physical Medicine and Rehabilitation* 76: 508–15.

Glanz M, Klawansky S, Stason W, *et al*, (1996) Functional electrostimulation in post-stroke rehabilitation: a meta-analysis of the randomised controlled trials. *Archives of Physical Medicine and Rehabilitation* 77: 549–53.

Glasgow RE, Toobert DJ, Hampson SE (1996) Effects of a brief office-based intervention to facilitate diabetes dietary self-management. *Diabetes Care* 19: 835–42.

Glasgow RE, La Chance PA, Toobert DJ, *et al*, (1997) Long term effects and costs of brief behavioural dietary intervention for patients with diabetes delivered from the medical office. *Patient Education and Counselling* 32: 175–84.

Glennon TP, Smith BS (1990) Questions asked by patients and their support groups during family conferences on inpatient rehabilitation units. *Archives of Physical Medicine and Rehabilitation* 71: 699–702.

Goldstein LB (1995) Common drugs may influence motor recovery after stroke. The Sygen In Acute Stroke Study Investigators. *Neurology* 45: 865–71.

Goldstein LB (1998) Accuracy of ICD-9-CM coding for the identification of patients with acute ischaemic stroke: effect of modifier codes. *Stroke*: 29: 1602–4.

Gompertz P, Pound P, Briffa J, Ebrahim S (1995) How useful are non-random comparisons of outcomes and quality of care in purchasing hospital stroke services. *Age and Ageing* 24: 137–41.

Gosman-Hedstrom G, Claesson L, Klingenstierna U, *et al*, (1998) Effects of acupuncture treatment on daily life activities and quality of life: a controlled prospective and randomised study of acute stroke patients. *Stroke* 29: 2100–8.

Grade C, Redford B, Chrostowski J, *et al*, (1998) Methylphenidate in early poststroke recovery: a double-blind, placebo-controlled study. *Archives Physical Medicine and Rehabilitation* 79: 1047–50.

Gray JM, Robertson I, Pentland B, Anderson S (1992) Microcomputer-based attentional retraining after brain damage: a randomised group controlled trial. *Neuropsychological Rehabilitation* 2(2): 97–115.

Grazko MA, Polo KB, Jabbari B (1995) Botulinum toxin A for spasticity, muscle spasms, and rigidity. *Neurology* 45: 712–7.

Greenberg S, Fowler RS (1980) Kinesthetic biofeedback: a treatment modality for elbow range of motion in hemiplegia. *American Journal of Occupational Therapy* 34: 738–743

Greener J, Enderby P, Whurr R (1999) Speech and language therapy for aphasia following stroke (Cochrane Review). In: The Cochrane Library, Issue 4, 1999. Oxford: Update Software.

Greenfield S, Kaplan S, Ware JE (1985) Expanding patient involvement in care. Effects on patient outcomes. *Annals of Internal Medicine* 102: 520–8.

Gross JC (1998) A comparison of the characteristics of incontinent and continent stroke patients in a rehabilitation programme. *Rehabilitation Nursing* 23: 132–40.

Gubitz G, Counsell C, Sandercock P, Signorini D (1999) Anticoagulants for acute ischaemic stroke (Cochrane Review). In: The Cochrane Library, Issue 3, 1999. Oxford: Update Software.

Gupta SR, Mlcoch AG, Scolaro C, Moritz T (1995) Bromocriptine treatment of nonfluent aphasia. *Neurology* 45: 2170–73.

Hakim EA, Bakheit AMO (1998) A study of the factors which influence the length of hospital stay of stroke patients. *Clinical Rehabilitation* **12**: 151–6.

Hansen R (1990) Social intervention at discharge: co-operation between a hospital department, general practice and the social sector. *Ugeskrift for Laeger.* **152**: 2506–10.

Harwood RH, Gompertz P, Ebrahim S (1994) Handicap one year after a stroke: validity of a new scale. *Journal of Neurology, Neurosurgery and Psychiatry* **57**: 825–9.

Hass U, Freden-Karlsson I, Persson J (1996) Assistive technologies in stroke rehabilitation from a user perspective. *Scandinavian Journal of Caring Sciences* **10**: 75–80.

Health & Safety Executive (1992) Manual handling: guidance on regulations. Sudbury, Suffolk: HSE.

Hebert PR, Gaziano JM, Chan KS, Hennekens CH (1997) Cholesterol lowering with statin drugs, risk of stroke and total mortality: an overview of randomised trials. *Journal of the American Medical Association* **278**: 313–21.

Hesse S, Bertelt C, Schaffrin A, *et al*, (1994) Restoration of gait in non-ambulatory hemiparetic patients by treadmill training with partial body-weight support. *Archives of Physical Medicine and Rehabilitation* **75**: 1087–93.

Hesse S, Bertelt C, Jahnke MT, *et al*, (1995a) Treadmill training with partial body weight support compared with physiotherapy in non-ambulatory hemiparetic patients. *Stroke* **26**: 976–81.

Hesse S, Malezic M, Schaffrin A, Mauritz KH (1995b) Restoration of gait by combined treadmill training and multi-channel electrical stimulation in non-ambulatory hemiparetic patients. *Scandinavian Journal of Rehabilitation Medicine* 27: 199–204.

Hesse S, Krajnik J, Luecke D, *et al*, (1996a) Ankle muscle activity before and after botulinum toxin therapy for lower limb extensor spasticity in chronic hemiparetic patients. *Stroke* **27**: 455–60.

Hesse S, Gahein-Sama AL, Mauritz KH (1996b) Technical aids in hemiparetic patients: prescription costs and usage. *Clinical Rehabilitation* **10**: 328–33.

Hesse S, Reiter F, Konrad M, Jahnke MT (1998) Botulinum toxin type A and short-term electrical stimulation in the treatment of upper limb flexor spasticity after stroke: a randomised, double-blind, placebo-controlled trial. *Clinical Rehabilitation* **12**: 381–8.

Holmqvist L, von Koch L, Kostulas V, *et al*, (1998) A randomised controlled trial of rehabilitation at home after stroke in southwest Stockholm. *Stroke* **29**: 591–7.

Horner J, Brazer SR, Massey EW (1993) Aspiration in bilateral stroke patients: a validation study. *Archives of Neurology* **43**: 430–3.

Hu HH, Chung C, Liu TJ, *et al*, (1993) A randomised controlled trial on the treatment for acute partial ischaemic stroke with acupuncture. *Neuroepidemiology* **12**: 106–13.

Huber W, Willmes K, Poeck K, *et al*, (1997) Piracetam as an adjuvant to language therapy for aphasia: a randomised double-blind placebo-controlled pilot study. *Archives of Physical Medicine and Rehabilitation* **78**: 245–50.

Huck J, Bonhotal BH (1997) Fastener systems on apparel for hemiplegic stroke victims. *Applied Ergonomics* **28**: 277–82.

Hui E, Lum CM, Woo J, *et al*, (1995) Outcomes of elderly stroke patients: day hospital versus conventional medical management. *Stroke* **26**: 1616–9.

Hurd WW, Pegram V, Nepomuceno C (1980) Comparison of actual and simulated EMG biofeedback in the treatment of hemiplegic patients. *American Journal of Physical Medicine* **59**: 73–82.

Indredavik B, Slordahl SA, Bakke F, *et al*, (1997) Stroke unit treatment. Long-term effects. *Stroke* **28**: 1861–6.

Indredavik B, Bakke F, Slordahl SA, *et al*, (1998) Stroke unit treatment improves long-term quality of life: a randomised controlled trial. *Stroke* **29**: 895–9.

Inglis J, Donald MW, Monga TN, *et al*, (1984) Electromyographic biofeedback and physical therapy of the hemiplegic upper limb. *Archives of Physical Medicine and Rehabilitation* **65**: 755–9.

Intercollegiate Working Party for Stroke (2000). A clinical audit package for stroke (2nd edn). London: Royal College of Physicians. In press

International Stroke Trial Collaborative Group (ISTCG) (1997) The International Stroke Trial (IST): a randomised trial of aspirin, subcutaneous heparin, both, or neither among 19,435 patients with acute ischaemic stroke. *Lancet* **349**: 1569–81.

Intiso D, Santilli V, Grasso MG, *et al*, (1994) Rehabilitation of walking with electromyographic biofeedback in foot-drop after stroke. *Stroke* **25**: 1189–92.

Jessee WF, Schranz CM (1990) Medicare mortality rates and hospital quality: are they related? *Quality Assurance in Health Care* **2**: 137–144

Johansson K, Lindgren I, Widner H, *et al*, (1993) Can sensory stimulation improve the functional outcome in stroke patients? *Neurology* **43**: 2189–92.

John J (1986) Failure of electrical myo-feedback to augment the effects of physiotherapy in stroke. *International Journal of Rehabilitation Research* **9**: 35–45.

Johnson L, Graham S, Harris KR (1997) The effects of goal setting and self-instruction on learning a reading comprehension strategy: a study of students with learning disabilities. *Journal of Learning Disabilities* **30**: 80–91.

Jones A, Carr EK, Newham DJ, Wilson-Barnett J (1998) Positioning of stroke patients. Evaluation of a teaching intervention with nurses. *Stroke* **29**: 1612–7.

Jongbloed L, Stacey S, Brighton C (1989) Stroke rehabilitation: sensorimotor integrative treatment versus functional treatment. *American Journal of Occupational Therapy* **43**: 391–7.

Jongbloed L, Morgan D (1991) An investigation of involvement in leisure activities after stroke. *American Journal of Occupational Therapy* **45**: 420–7.

Kalra L (1994) The influence of stroke unit rehabilitation on functional recovery from stroke. *Stroke* **25**: 821–5.

Kalra L, Perez I, Gupta S, Wittink M (1997). The influence of visual neglect on stroke rehabilitation. *Stroke* **28**: 1386–91.

Katrak PH, Cole AM, Poulos CJ, McCauley JC (1992) Objective assessment of spasticity, strength, and function with early exhibition of dantrolene sodium after cerebrovascular accident: a randomised, double-blind study. *Archives of Physical Medicine and Rehabilitation* **73**: 4–9.

Katz RC, Wertz RT (1997) The efficacy of computer-provided reading treatment for chronic aphasic adults. *Journal of Speech, Language and Hearing Research* **40**: 493–507.

Kawachi I, Colditz GA, Stamper MJ, *et al*, (1993) Smoking cessation and decreased risk of stroke in women. *Journal of the American Medical Association* **269**: 232–6.

Kelson M, Ford C, Rigge M (1998) Stroke rehabilitation: patient and carer views. A report by the College of Health for the Intercollegiate Working Party for Stroke. London: Royal College of Physicians.

Kennedy AP, Brocklehurst JC (1982) The nursing management of patients with long-term in-dwelling catheters. *Journal of Advanced Nursing* **7**: 411–7.

Kennedy AP, Brocklehurst JC, Lye MDW (1983) Factors related to the problems of long-term catheterisation. *Journal of Advanced Nursing* **8**: 207–12.

Kennedy L, Neidlinger S, Scroggins K (1987) Effective comprehensive discharge planning for hospitalised elderly. *Gerontologist* **27**: 577–80.

Kennedy P, Walker L, White D (1991) Ecological evaluation of goal planning and advocacy in a rehabilitation environment for spinal cord injured people. *Paraplegia* **29**: 197–202.

Kerkhoff G, Munssinger U, Meier EK (1994) Neurovisual rehabilitation in cerebral blindness. *Archives of Neurology* **51**: 474–81.

Ketel WB, Kolb ME (1984) Long-term treatment with dantrolene sodium of stroke patients with spasticity limiting the return of function. *Current Medical Research and Opinion* **9**: 161–9.

Kidd D, Lawson J, Nesbit R, MacMahon J (1993) Aspiration in acute stroke: a clinical study with videofluoroscopy. *Quarterly Journal of Medicine* **86**: 825–9.

Kjendahl A, Sallstrom S, Osten PE, *et al*, (1997) A one year follow-up study on the effects of acupuncture in the treatment of stroke patients in the subacute stage. *Clinical Rehabilitation* **11**: 192–200.

Kollef MH, Shapiro SD, Silver P, *et al*, (1997) A randomised, controlled trial of protocol-directed versus physician-directed weaning from mechanical ventilation. *Critical Care Medicine* **25**: 567–74.

Kothari R, Barsan W, Brott T, *et al*, (1995a) Frequency and accuracy of prehospital diagnosis of stroke. *Stroke* **26**: 937–41.

Kothari R, Brott T, Broderick J, Hamilton CA (1995b) Emergency physicians' accuracy in the diagnosis of stroke. *Stroke* **26**: 2238–41.

Kothari R, Hall K, Brott T, Broderick J (1997) Early stroke recognition: developing an out-of-hospital NIH stroke scale. *Academic Emergency Medicine* **4**: 986–990.

Kotzki N, Pelissier J, Dusotoit C, *et al*, (1991) Techniques de prévention du syndrome algodystrophique: évaluation d'un protocole d'installation au lit. *Annales Réadaptation Médicine Physique* **34**: 351–5.

Koudstaal P (1995a) Anticoagulants for preventing stroke in patients with non-rheumatic atrial fibrillation and a history of stroke or transient ischaemic attacks (Cochrane Review). In: The Cochrane Library, Issue 3, 1999. Oxford: Update Software.

Koudstaal P (1995b) Anti-platelet therapy for preventing stroke in patients with non-rheumatic atrial fibrillation and a history of stroke or transient ischaemic attacks (Cochrane Review). In: The Cochrane Library, Issue 3, 1999. Oxford: Update Software.

Kraaijeveld CL, van Gijn J, Schouten HJA, Staal A (1984) Inter-observer agreement for the diagnosis of transient ischaemic attacks. *Stroke* **15**: 723–5.

Kumar R, Metter EJ, Mehta AJ, Chew T (1990) Shoulder pain in hemiplegia: The role of exercise. *American Journal of Physical Medicine and Rehabilitation* **69**: 205–8.

Kuntz KM, Kent C (1996) Is carotid endarterectomy cost-effective? An analysis of symptomatic and asymptomatic patients. *Stroke* **94** (Suppl II): II-194, II-198.

Kwakkel G, Wagenaar RC, Koelman TW, *et al*, (1997) Effects of intensity of rehabilitation after stroke: a research synthesis. *Stroke* **28**: 1550–6.

Kwakkel G, Wagenaar RC, Twisk JWR, *et al*, (1999) Intensity of leg and arm training after primary middle-cerebral-artery stroke: a randomised trial. *Lancet* **354**: 191–6.

Landefeld CS, Palmer RM, Kresevic DM, *et al*, (1995) A randomised trial of care in a hospital medical unit especially designed to improve the functional outcomes of acutely ill older patients. *New England Journal of Medicine* **332**: 1338–44

Langhorne P, Wagenaar R, Partridge C (1996) Physiotherapy after stroke: more is better? *Physiotherapy Research International* **1**: 75–88.

Langhorne P, Dennis M, Kalra L, *et al*, (1999) Services for helping acute stroke patients avoid hospital admission (Cochrane Review). In: The Cochrane Library, Issue 3, 1999. Oxford: Update Software.

Laursen SO, Henriksen IO, Dons U, *et al*, (1995) Intensiv apopleksirehabilitering – et kontrolleret pilotstudie. *Ugeskrift for Laeger* **157**: 1996–9.

Lawson IR, MacLeod RD (1969) The use of imipramine (Tofranil) and other psychotropic drugs in organic emotionalism. *British Journal of Psychiatry* **115**: 281–5.

Leandri M, Parodi CI, Corrieri N, Rigard S (1990) Comparison of TENS treatments in hemiplegic shoulder pain. *Scandanavian Journal of Rehabilitation Medicine* **22**: 69–72.

Lee KH, Hill E, Johnston R, Smiehorowski T (1976) Myo-feedback for muscle retraining in hemiplegic patients. *Archives of Physical Medicine and Rehabilitation* **57**: 588–91.

Lee AJ, Huber JH, Stason WB (1997) Factors contributing to practice variation in post-stroke rehabilitation. *Health Services Research* **32**: 197–221.

Lehman JF, DeLateur BJ, Fowler RS, *et al*, (1975) Stroke: does rehabilitation affect outcome? *Archives of Physical Medicine and Rehabilitation* **56**: 375–82.

Leibson CL, Naessens JM, Brown RD, Whisnant JP (1994) Accuracy of hospital discharge abstracts for identifying stroke. *Stroke* **25**: 2348–55.

Leijon G, Boivie J (1989) Central post-stroke pain: a controlled trial of amitriptyline and carbamazepine. *Pain* **36**: 27–36.

Lemesle M, Madinier G, Menassa M, *et al*, (1998) Incidence of transient ischaemic attacks in Dijon, France: a 5-year community-based study. *Neuroepidemiology* **17**: 74–9.

Lennard-Jones JE (Ed) (1992). A positive approach to nutrition as treatment. London: King's Fund Centre.

Levy DE (1988) Transient CNS deficits: a common, benign syndrome in young adults. *Neurology* **38**: 831–6.

Lightowlers S, McGuire A (1998) Cost-effectiveness of anticoagulation in nonrheumatic atrial fibrillation in the primary prevention of ischaemic stroke. *Stroke* **29**: 1827–32.

Lilford RJ, Kelly M, Baines A, *et al*, (1992) Effects of using protocols on medical care: randomised trial of three methods of taking an antenatal history. *British Medical Journal* **305**: 1181–4.

Lincoln NB, Whiting SE, Cockburn J, Bhavnani G (1985) An evaluation of perceptual retraining. *International Rehabilitation Medicine* **7**: 99–110.

Lincoln NB, Willis D, Philips SA, *et al*, (1996) Comparison of rehabilitation practice on hospital wards for stroke patients. *Stroke* **27**: 18–23.

Lincoln NB, Drummond AER, Berman P (1997) Perceptual impairment and its impact on rehabilitation outcome. *Disability and Rehabilitation* **19**: 231–4.

Lincoln NB, Parry RH, Vass CD (1999) Randomized, controlled trial to evaluate increased intensity of physiotherapy treatment of arm function after stroke. *Stroke* **30**: 573–79.

Lindley RI, Warlow CP, Wardlaw JM, *et al*, (1993) Inter-observer reliability of a clinical classification of acute cerebral infarction. *Stroke* **24**: 1801–4.

Lindley RI, Waddell F, Livingstone M, *et al*, (1994) Can simple questions assess outcome after stroke? *Cerebrovascular Disease* **4**: 314–24.

Linn SL, Granat MH, Lees KR (1999) Prevention of shoulder subluxation after stroke with electrical stimulation. *Stroke* **30**: 963–8.

Lipsey JR, Robinson RG, Pearlson GD, *et al*, (1984) Nortriptyline treatment of post-stroke depression: a double-blind study. *Lancet* **1**: 297–300.

Liu M, Wardlaw J (1996) Fibrinogen depleting agents for acute ischaemic stroke (Cochrane Review). In: The Cochrane Library, Issue 3, 1999. Oxford: Update Software.

Liu M, Wardlaw J. (1998) Thrombolysis (different doses, routes of administration and agents) for acute ischaemic stroke (Cochrane Review). In: The Cochrane Library, Issue 3, 1999. Oxford: Update Software.

Liu M, Counsell C, Sandercock P (1997) Anticoagulation for preventing recurrence following ischaemic stroke or transient ischaemic attack (Cochrane Review). In: The Cochrane Library, Issue 3, 1999. Oxford: Update Software.

Logan PA, Ahern J, Gladman JRF, Lincoln NB (1997) A randomised controlled trial of enhanced social services occupational therapy for stroke patients. *Clinical Rehabilitation* **11**: 107–13.

Logigian MK, Samuels MA, Falconer J (1983) Clinical exercise trial for stroke patients. *Archives of Physical Medicine and Rehabilitation* **64**: 364–7.

Lomer M, McLellan DL (1987) Informing hospital patients and their relatives about stroke. *Clinical Rehabilitation* **1**: 33–7

Lord JP, Hall K (1986) Neuromuscular re-education versus traditional programs for stroke rehabilitation. *Archives of Physical Medicine and Rehabilitation* **67**: 88–91.

Lu CL, Yu B, Basford JR, *et al*, (1997) Influences of cane length on the stability of stroke patients. *Journal of Rehabilitation Research and Development* **34**: 91–100.

Lyon JG, Cariski D, Keisler L, *et al*, (1997) Communication partners: enhancing participation in life and communication for adults with aphasia in natural settings. *Aphasiology* **11**: 693-708.

McCollum PT, da Silva A, Ridler BDM, de Cossart L, and the Audit Committee (1997) Carotid endarterectomy in the U.K. and Ireland: audit of 30-day outcome. *European Journal of Vascular and Endovascular Surgery* **14**: 386–91.

McGrath JR, Davies AM (1992) Rehabilitation: where are we going and how do we get there? *Clinical Rehabilitation* **6**: 225–35.

McGrath JR, Marks JA, Davies AM (1995) Towards inter-disciplinary rehabilitation: further developments at Rivermead Rehabilitation Centre. *Clinical Rehabiliation* **9**: 320–6.

Mackenzie C (1991) An aphasia group intensive efficacy study. *British Journal of Disorders of Communication* **26**: 275–91.

Macko RF, DeSouza CA, Tretter LD, *et al*, (1997) Treadmill aerobic exercise training reduces the energy expenditure and cardiovascular demands of hemiparetic gait in chronic stroke patients: a preliminary report. *Stroke* **28**: 326–30.

McNaughton H (1996) Stroke audit in a New Zealand hospital. *New Zealand Medical Journal* **109**: 257–60

Madden KP, Karanjia PN, Adams HP, Clarke WR, and the TOAST investigators (1995) Accuracy of initial stroke subtype diagnosis in the TOAST study. *Neurology* **45**: 1975–9.

Malouin F, Potvon M, Prevost J, *et al*, (1992) Use of an intensive task-oriented gait training program in a series of patients with acute cerebrovascular accidents. *Physical Therapy* **72**: 781–93.

Mamon J, Steinwachs DM, Fahey M, *et al*, (1992) Impact of hospital discharge planning on meeting patient needs after returning home. *Health Services Research* **27**: 155–75.

Mandel AR, Nymark JR, Balmer SJ, *et al*, (1990) Electromyographic versus rhythmic positional biofeedback in computerised gait retraining with stroke patients. *Archives of Physical Medicine and Rehabilitation* **71**: 649–54.

Mann WC, Hurren D, Tomita M and Charvat B (1995) Assistive devices for home-based older stroke survivors. *Topics in Geriatric Rehabilitation* **10**: 75–86.

Mann WC, Ottenbacher KJ, Fraas L, *et al*, (1999) Effectiveness of assistive technology and environmental interventions in maintaining independence and reducing home care costs for the elderly. *Archives of Family Medicine* **8**: 210–7.

Mant J, Hicks N (1995) Detecting differences in quality of care: the sensitivity of measures of process and outcome in treating myocardial infarction. *British Medical Journal* 311: 793–6.

Mant J, Mant F, Winner S (1997) How good is routine information? Validation of coding for acute stroke in Oxford hospitals. *Health Trends* **29**: 96–9.

Mant J, Carter J, Wade DT, Winner S (1998) The impact of an information pack on patients with stroke and their carers: a randomised controlled trial. *Clinical Rehabilitation* **12**: 465–76.

Marshall EC, Spiegelhalter DJ (1998) Reliability of league tables of in vitro fertilisation clinics: retrospective analysis of live birth rates. *British Medical Journal* **316**: 1701–5.

Martin PJ, Young G, Enevoldson TP, Humphrey PRD (1997) Overdiagnosis of TIA and minor stroke: experience at a regional neurovascular clinic. *Quarterly Journal of Medicine* **90**: 759–63.

Mathew P, Teasdale G, Bannan A, Oluoch-Olunya (1995) Neurological management of cerebellar haematoma and infarct. *Journal of Neurology Neurosurgery and Psychiatry* **59**: 287–92.

Mathias SD, Bates MM, Pasta DJ, *et al*, (1997) Use of the Health Utilities Index with stroke patients and their caregivers. *Stroke* **28**: 1888–94.

Medici M, Pebet M, Ciblis D (1989) A double-blind, long-term study of tizanidine (Sirdalud) in spasticity due to cerebrovascular lesions. *Current Medical Research and Opinion* **11**: 398–407.

Midgley JP, Matthew AG, Greenwood CM, Logan AG (1996) Effect of reduced dietary sodium on blood pressure: a meta-analysis of randomised controlled trials. *Journal of the American Medical Association* **275**: 1590–7.

Miller GJT, Light KE (1997) Strength training in spastic hemiparesis: should it be avoided? *NeuroRehabilitation* **9**: 17–28.

Miyai I, Reding MJ (1998) Effects of anti-depressants on functional recovery following stroke: a double-blind study. *Journal of Neurologic Rehabilitation* **12**: 5–13.

Mohiuddin AA, Bath FJ, Bath PMW (1999) Theophylline, aminophylline, caffeine and analogues for acute ischaemic stroke (Cochrane Review). In: The Cochrane Library, Issue 3, 1999. Oxford: Update Software.

Montoya R, Dupui P, Pages B, Bessou P (1994) Step-length biofeedback device for walk rehabilitation. *Medical Biological Engineering and Computing* **32**: 416–20.

Moore WS, Young B, Baker WH, *et al*, and the ACAS investigators (1996) Surgical results: a justification of the surgeon selection process for the ACAS trial. *Journal of Vascular Surgery* **23**: 323–8.

Moreland J, Thomson MA (1994) Efficacy of electromyographic biofeedback compared with conventional physical therapy for upper-extremity function in patients following stroke: a research overview and meta-analysis. *Physical Therapy* **74**: 534–47.

Moreland JD, Thomson MA, Fuoco AR (1998) Electromyographic biofeedback to improve lower extremity function after stroke: a meta-analysis. *Archives of Physical Medicine and Rehabilitation* **79**: 134–40.

Morris ME, Matyas TA, Back TM, Goldie PA (1992) Electrogoniometric feedback: its effect on genu recurvatum in stroke. *Archives of Physical Medicine and Rehabilitation* **73**: 1147–54.

Multi-centre Acute Stroke Trial – Italy (MAST-I) (1995) Randomised controlled trial of streptokinase, aspirin and combination of both in treatment of acute ischaemic stroke. *Lancet* **346**: 1508–14.

Nakayama H, Jorgensen HS, Pedersen PM, *et al*, (1997) Prevalence and risk factors of incontinence after stroke: the Copenhagen Stroke Study. *Stroke* **28**: 58-62.

Naylor MD (1990) Comprehensive discharge planning for hospitalised elderly: a pilot study. *Nursing Research* **39**: 156–61.

Naylor M, Brooten D, Jones R, *et al*, (1994) Comprehensive discharge planning for the hospitalised elderly: a randomised clinical trial. *Annals of Internal Medicine* **120**: 999–1006.

Neidlinger S, Scroggins K, Kennedy L (1987) Cost evaluation of discharge planning for hospitalised elderly. *Nursing Economics* **5**: 225–230

Nelson DL, Konosky K, Fleharty K, *et al*, (1996) The effects of an occupationally embedded exercise on bilaterally assisted supination in persons with hemiplegia. *American Journal of Occupational Therapy* **50**: 639–46.

Neville DU, Piersol CV, Keilhofner G, Davis K (1993) Adaptive equipment: a study of utilization after hospital discharge. *Occupational Therapy in Health Care* **8**: 3–18.

Norris JW, Hachinski VC (1982) Misdiagnosis of stroke. *Lancet* **1**: 328–31.

North American Symptomatic Carotid Endarterectomy Trial Collaborators (NASCET) (1998) Benefit of carotid endarterectomy in patients with symptomatic moderate or severe stenosis. *New England Journal of Medicine* **337**: 1415–25.

Norton B, Homer-Ward M, Donnelly MT, *et al*, (1996) A randomised prospective comparison of percutaneous endoscopic gastrostomy and nasogastric tube feeding after acute dysphagic stroke. *British Medical Journal* **312**: 13–6.

Nouri FM, Lincoln NB (1993) Predicting diving performance stroke. *British Medical Journal* **307**: 482–3.

Nussbaum ES, Heros RC, Erickson DL (1996) Cost-effectiveness of carotid endarterectomy. *Neurosurgery* **38**: 237–44.

Odderson IR, Keaton JC, McKenna BS (1995) Swallow management in patients on an acute stroke pathway: quality is cost effective. *Archives of Physical Medicine and Rehabilitation* **76**: 1130–3.

O'Mahony PG, Rodgers H, Thomson RG, *et al*, (1997) Satisfaction with information and advice received by stroke patients. *Clinical Rehabilitation* **11**: 68–72.

O'Mahony PG, Rodgers H, Thomson RG, *et al*, (1998) Is the SF-36 suitable for assessing health status of older stroke patients? *Age and Ageing* **27**: 19–22.

O'Rourke S, MacHale S, Signorini D, Dennis M (1998) Detecting psychiatric morbidity after stroke: comparison of the GHQ and the HAD scale. *Stroke* **29**: 980–5.

Pain HSB, McLellan DL (1990) The use of individualised booklets after *stroke. Clinical Rehabilitation* **4**: 265–72.

Palomaki H, Kaste M, Berg A, *et al*, (1999) Prevention of post-stroke depression: one year randomised placebo controlled double blind trial of mianserin with 6 month follow up after therapy. *Journal of Neurology Neurosurgery and Psychiatry* **66**: 490–4.

Parfrey PS, Gardner E, Vavasour H, *et al*, (1994) The feasibility and efficacy of early discharge planning initiated by the admitting department in two acute care hospitals. *Clinical and Investigative Medicine* **17**: 88–96.

Parry RH, Lincoln NB, Vass CD (1999) Effect of arm impairment on response to additional physiotherapy after stroke. *Clinical Rehabilitation* **13**: 187–98.

Partridge CJ, Edwards SM, Mee R, van Langenberghe HVK (1990) Hemiplegic shoulder pain: a study of two methods of physiotherapy treatment. *Clinical Rehabilitation* **4**: 43–9.

Patel M, Potter J, Perez I, Kalra L (1998) The process of rehabilitation and discharge planning in stroke: a controlled comparison between stroke units. *Stroke* **29**: 2484–7.

Penman JP, Thomson M (1998) A review of the textured diets developed for the management of dysphagia. *Journal of Human Nutrition and Dietetics* **11**: 51–60.

Perez I, Smithard DG, Davies H, Kalra L (1998) Pharmacological treatment of dysphagia in stroke. *Dysphagia* **13**: 12–16

Poeck K, Humer W, Wilmess K (1989) Outcome of intensive language treatment in aphasia. *Aphasiology* **54**: 471–9.

Poloniecki J (1998) Half of all doctors are below average. *British Medical Journal* **316**: 1734–6.

Poloniecki J, Valencia O, Littlejohns P (1998) Cumulative risk adjusted mortality chart for detecting changes in death rate: observational study of heart surgery. *British Medical Journal* **316**: 1697–1700.

Post MWM, de Witte LP, Schrijvers AJP (1999) Quality of life and the ICIDH: towards an integrated conceptual model for rehabilitation outcomes research. *Clinical Rehabilitation* **13**: 5–15.

Post-stroke Antihypertensive Treatment Study (PATS) Collaborative Group (1995) Post Stroke Antihypertensive Treatment Study: a preliminary result. *Chinese Medical Journal* **108**: 710–7.

Potter J, Langhorne P, Roberts M (1998) Routine protein energy supplementation in adults: systematic review. *British Medical Journal* **317**: 495–501.

Pound P, Gompertz P, Ebrahim S (1998) A patient-centred study of the consequences of stroke. *Clinical Rehabilitation*; **12**: 338–347

Pound P, Tilling K, Rudd AG, Wolfe CDA (1999) Does patient satisfaction reflect differences in care received after stroke? *Stroke* **30**: 49–55.

Powell J, Pandyan AD, Granat M, *et al*, (1999) Electrical stimulation of wrist extensors in post-stroke hemiplegia. *Stroke* **30**: 1384–9.

Prasad K, Shrivastava A (1998) Surgery for primary supratentorial intracerebral haemorrhage (Cochrane Review). In: The Cochrane Library, Issue 3, 1999. Oxford: Update Software.

Prevo AJH, Visser SL, Vogelaar TW (1982) Effect of EMG biofeedback on paretic muscles and abnormal co-contraction in the hemiplegic arm compared with conventional physical therapy. *Scandinavian Journal of Rehabilitation Medicine* **14**: 121–31.

Qizilbash N, Lewington SL, Lopez-Arrieta JM (1998) Corticosteroids for acute ischaemic stroke (Cochrane Review) In: The Cochrane Library, Issue 3, 1999. Oxford: Update Software.

Raffaele R, Rompello L, Vecchio I, *et al*, (1996) Trazodone therapy of post-stroke depression. *Archives of Gerontology and Geriatrics Suppl* **5**: 217–20.

Ramsay LE, Williams B, Johnston DG, *et al*, (1999) Guidelines for management of hypertension: report of the third working party of the British Hypertension Society. *Journal of Human Hypertension* **13**: 569–92.

Rapoport J, Eerd MJ (1989) Impact of physical therapy weekend coverage on length of stay in an acute care community hospital. *Physical Therapy* **69**: 32–7.

Reding MJ, Orto LA, Winter SW, *et al*, (1986) Anti-depressant therapy after stroke: a double blind study. *Archives of Neurology* **43**: 763–5.

Reilly HM (1996) Screening for nutritional risk. *Proceedings of the Nutrition Society* **55**: 841–53.

Reiter F, Danni M, Lagalla G, *et al*, (1998) Low-dose botulinum toxin with ankle taping for the treatment of spastic equinovarus foot after stroke. *Archives of Physical Medicine and Rehabilitation* **79**: 532–5.

Ricci S, Celani MG, La Rosa F, *et al*, (1991) SEPIVAC: a community based study of stroke incidence in Umbria, Italy. *Journal of Neurology, Neurosurgery and Psychiatry* **54**: 695–8.

Ricci S, Celani MG, Cantisani AT, Righetti E (1999) Piracetam for acute ischaemic stroke (Cochrane Review). In: The Cochrane Library, Issue 3, 1999. Oxford: Update Software.

Rice P, Paull A, Muller D (1987) An evaluation of a social support group for spouses of aphasic partners. *Aphasiology* **1**: 247–56.

Richards CL, Malouin F, Wood-Dauphinee S, *et al*, (1993) Task-specific physical therapy for optimisation of gait recovery in acute stroke patients. *Archives of Physical Medicine and Rehabilitation* **74**: 612–20.

Richards SH, Coast J, Gunnell DJ, *et al*, (1998) Randomised controlled trial comparing effectiveness and acceptability of an early discharge, hospital at home scheme with acute hospital care. *British Medical Journal* **316**: 1796–1801.

Rigby D (1998) Long-term catheter care. *Professional Nurse Study Supplement* **13**: S14–S15.

Robey R (1994) The efficacy of treatment for asphasic persons: a meta-analysis. *Brain and Language* **47**: 582–608.

Robey R (1998) A meta-analysis of clinical outcomes in the treatment of aphasia. *Journal of Speech and Hearing Research* **41**: 172–187

Robinson RG, Parikh RM, Lipsey JR, *et al*, (1993) Pathological laughing and crying following stroke: validation of a measurement scale and a double blind treatment study. *American Journal of Psychiatry* **150**: 286–93.

Rockwood K, Stolee P, Fox RA (1993) Use of goal attainment scaling in measuring clinically important change in the frail elderly. *Journal of Clinical Epidemiology* **46**: 1113–8.

Rockwood K, Joyce B, Stolee P (1997) Use of goal attainment scaling in measuring clinically important change in cognitive rehabilitation patients. *Journal of Clinical Epidemiology* **50**: 581–8.

Rodgers H, Soutter J, Kaiser W, *et al*, (1997) Early supported discharge following acute stroke: pilot study results. *Clinical Rehabilitation* **11**: 280–7.

Ronning OM, Guldvog B (1998a) Stroke unit versus general medical wards, II: neurological deficits and activities of daily living. A quasi-randomised controlled trial. *Stroke* **29**: 586–90.

Ronning OM, Guldvog B (1998b) Outcome of subacute stroke rehabilitation: a randomized controlled trial. *Stroke* **29**: 779-84.

Ronning OM, Guldvog B (1999) Should stroke victims routinely receive supplemented oxygen? A quasi-randomised controlled trial. *Stroke* **30**: 2033–7.

Royal College of Physicians (1995) Incontinence: causes, management and provision of services. A report of the Royal College of Physicians. London: RCP.

Royal College of Physicians (1998) Promoting continence: clinical audit scheme for the management of urinary and faecal incontinence. London: RCP.

Royal College of Physicians of Edinburgh (1998) Royal College of Physicians of Edinburgh Consensus Conference on Medical Management of Stroke, 26–27 May 1998. *Age and Ageing* **27**: 665–6.

Royal College of Radiologists (1998) Making the best use of a department of clinical radiology: guidelines for doctors. 4th edition.

Rudd AG, Wolfe CD, Tilling K, Beech R (1997) Randomised controlled trial to evaluate early discharge scheme for patients with stroke. *British Medical Journal* **315**: 1039–44.

Rudd AG, Irwin P, Rutledge Z, *et al*, (1999) The national sentinel audit of stroke: a tool for raising standards of care. *J R Coll Physicians Lond* **33**: 460–4.

Sabe L, Salvarezza F, Garcia Cuerva A, *et al*, (1995) A randomised, double-blind, placebo-controlled study of bromocriptine in nonfluent aphasia. *Neurology* **45**: 2272–4.

Sackley CM, Lincoln NB (1997) Single-blind randomised controlled trial of visual feedback after stroke: effects on stance symmetry and function. *Disability and Rehabilitation* **19**: 536–46.

Sagar G, Riley P, Vohrah A (1996) Is admission chest radiography of any clinical value in acute stroke patients? *Clinical Radiology* **51**: 499–502.

Sallstrom S, Kjendahl A, Osten PE, *et al*, (1996) Acupuncture in the treatment of stroke patients in the subacute stage: a randomised controlled study. *Complementary Therapies in Medicine* **4**: 193–7.

Sampaio C, Ferreira JJ, Pinto AA, *et al*, (1997) Botulinum toxin type A for the treatment of arm and hand spasticity in stroke patients. *Clinical Rehabilitation* **11**: 3–7.

Sandercock PAG, Allen CMC, Corston RN, *et al*, (1985) Clinical diagnosis of intracranial haemorrhage using Guy's Hospital score. *British Medical Journal* **291**: 1675–7.

Sarno MT, Sarno JE, Diller L (1972) The effect of hyperbaric oxygen on communication function in adults with aphasia secondary to stroke. *Journal of Speech and Hearing Research* **15**: 42–8.

Schauer M, Steingruber W, Mauritz K-H (1996) The effect of music on gait symmetry in stroke patients walking on the treadmill. *Biomedizinische Technik* **41**: 291–6.

Schiffer RB, Herndon RM, Rudick RA (1985) Treatment of pathologic laughing and weeping with amitriptyline. *New England Journal of Medicine* **312**: 1480–2.

Schleenbaker RE, Mainous AG (1993) Electromyographic biofeedback for neuromuscular re-education in the hemiplegic stroke patient: a meta-analysis. *Archives of Physical Medicine and Rehabilitation* **74**: 1301–4.

Scholte op Reimer WJM, de Haan RJ, van den Bos GAM (1996) Patients' satisfaction with care after stroke: relation with characteristics of patients and care. *Quality in Healthcare* **5**: 144–50.

Scholte op Reimer WJM, de Haan RJ, Pijnenborg JMA, *et al*, (1998a) Assessment of burden in partners of stroke patients with Sense of Competence Questionnaire. *Stroke* **29**: 373–9.

Scholte op Reimer WJM, de Haan RJ, Rijnders PT, *et al*, (1998b) The burden of caregiving in partners of long-term stroke survivors. *Stroke* **29**: 1605–11.

Schultz S, Castillo C, Kosner J, Robinson R (1997) Generalised anxiety and depression: assessment over 2 years after stroke. *American Journal of Geriatric Psychiatry* **5**: 229–37.

Scottish Intercollegiate Guidelines Network (SIGN) (1997a) Management of patients with Stroke. 1.Assessment, investigation, immediate management and secondary prevention. Edinburgh: SIGN. Publication No. 13.

Scottish Intercollegiate Guidelines Network (SIGN) (1997b) Management of patients with stroke, II. Management of carotid stenosis and carotid endarterectomy. SIGN. Edinburgh. Publication No. 14

Scottish Intercollegiate Guidelines Network (SIGN) (1997c) Management of patients with stroke, III. Identification and management of dysphagia. Edinburgh: SIGN. Publication No. 20.

Scottish Intercollegiate Guidelines Network (SIGN) (1998) Management of patients with stroke, IV. Rehabilitation, prevention and management of complications, and discharge planning. Edinburgh: SIGN. Publication No. 24.

Shah S, Vanclay F, Cooper B (1990) Efficiency, effectiveness and duration of stroke rehabilitation. *Stroke* **21**: 241–6.

Sharp SA, Brouwer BJ (1997) Isokinetic strength training of the hemiparetic knee: effects on function and spasticity. *Archives of Physical Medicine and Rehabilitation* **78**: 1231–6.

Shepperd S, Iliffe S (1997) Hospital-at-home versus in-patient hospital care (Cochrane Review). In: The Cochrane Library, Issue 2, 1999. Oxford: Update Software.

Shepperd S, Harwood D, Jenkinson C, *et al*, (1998a) Randomised controlled trial comparing hospital at home care with inpatient hospital care. I. Three month follow-up of health outcomes. *British Medical Journal* **316**: 1786–91.

Shepperd S, Harwood D, Gray A, *et al*, (1998b) Randomised controlled trial comparing hospital at home care with inpatient hospital care. II. Cost minimisation analysis. *British Medical Journal* **316**: 1791–6.

Shirran E, Brazzelli M (1999) Absorbent products for the containment of urinary and/or faecal incontinence in adults (Cochrane Review). In: The Cochrane Library, Issue 3,1999. Oxford: Update Software.

Simpson DM, Alexander DN, O'Brien CF, *et al*, (1996) Botulinum toxin type A in the treatment of upper extremity spasticity: a randomised, double-blind, placebo-controlled trial. *Neurology* **46**: 1306–10.

Smith KN (1979) Biofeedback in strokes. Australian Journal of Physiotherapy **25**: 155–61.

Smith DS, Goldenberg E, Ashburn A, *et al*, (1981a) Remedial therapy after stroke: a randomised controlled trial. *British Medical Journal* **282**: 517–20.

Smith ME, Walton MS, Garraway WM (1981b) The use of aids and adaptations in a study of stroke rehabilitation. *Health Bulletin (Edinburgh)* **39**: 98–106.

Smithard DG, O'Neill PA, Park C, *et al*, (1996) Complications and outcome after acute stroke: does dysphagia matter? *Stroke* **27**: 1200–4.

Sneeuw KCA, Aaronson NK, de Haan RJ, Limburg M (1997) Assessing quality of life after stroke: the value and limitations of proxy ratings. *Stroke* **28**: 1541–9.

Snow BJ, Tsui JKC, Bhatt MH, *et al*, (1990) Treatment of spasticity with botulinum toxin: a double-blind study. *Annals of Neurology* **28**: 512–5.

Sonde L, Fernaeus SE, Nilsson CG, Viitanen M (1998) Stimulation with low frequency (1.7 Hz) tanscutaneous electric nerve stimulation (Low-TENS) increases motor function of the post-stroke paretic arm. *Scandinavian Journal of Rehabilitation Medicine* **30**: 95–9.

Sonn U, Davegardh H, Lindskog AC, Steen B (1996) The use and effectiveness of assistive devices in an elderly urban population. *Ageing: Clinical and Experimental Research* **8**: 176–83.

Sotaniemi KA, Pyhtinen J, Myllyla VV (1990) Correlation of clinical and computed tomographic findings in stroke patients. *Stroke* **21**: 1562–6.

Splaingard ML, Hutchins B, Sulton LD, Chauduri G (1988) Aspiration in rehabilitation patients: videofluoroscopy vs bedside clinical assessment. *Archives of Physical Medicine and Rehabilitation* **69**: 637–40.

Stenstrom CH (1994) Home exercise in rheumatoid arthritis functional class II: goal setting versus pain attention. *Journal of Rheumatology* **21**: 627–34.

Stineman MG, Granger CV (1998) Outcome, efficiency, and time trend pattern analyses for stroke rehabilitation. *American Journal of Physical Medicine and Rehabilitation* **77**: 193–201.

Stolee P, Rockwood K, Fox RA, Streiner DL (1992) The use of goal attainment scaling in a geriatric care setting. *Journal of the American Geriatrics Society* **40**: 574–8.

Stroke Prevention in Atrial Fibrillation Investigators (1996) Adjusted-dose warfarin versus low-intensity, fixed-dose warfarin plus aspirin for high risk patients with atrial fibrillation: stroke prevention in atrial fibrillation III randomised clinical trial. *Lancet* **348**: 633–8.

Stroke Prevention in Reversible Ischaemia Trial (SPIRIT) Study Group (1997). A randomised trial of anticoagulants versus aspirin after cerebral ischaemia of presumed arterial origin. *Annals of Neurology* **42**: 857–65.

Stroke Unit Trialists' Collaboration (1998) Organised inpatient (stroke unit) care for stroke (Cochrane Review). In: The Cochrane Library, Issue 3, 1999. Oxford: Update Software.

Stuck AE, Siu AL, Wieland GD, *et al*, (1993) Comprehensive geriatric assessment: a meta-analysis of controlled trials. *Lancet* **342**: 1032–6.

Sukthankar SM, Reddy NP, Canilang EP, *et al*, (1994) Design and development of portable biofeedback systems for us in oral dysphagia rehabilitation. *Medical Engineering and Physics* **16**: 430–5.

Sunderland A, Tinson DJ, Bradley EL, *et al*, (1992) Enhanced physical therapy improves recovery of arm function after stroke: a randomised controlled trial. *Journal of Neurology, Neurosurgery and Psychiatry* **55**: 530–5.

Sunderland A, Fletcher D, Bradley L, *et al*, (1994) Enhanced physical therapy for arm function after stroke: a one year follow-up study. *Journal of Neurology, Neurosurgery and Psychiatry* **57**: 856–8.

Svensson BH, Christiansen LS, Jepsen E (1992) Treatment of central facial nerve paralysis with electromyography biofeedback and taping of cheek: a controlled clinical trial. *Ugeskrift for Laeger* **154**: 3593–6.

Tangeman PT, Banaitis DA, Williams AK (1990) Rehabilitation of chronic stroke patients: changes in functional performance. *Archives of Physical Medicine and Rehabilitation* **71**: 876–80.

Teasell RW, McRae M, Marchuk Y, Finestone HM (1996) Pneumonia associated with aspiration following stroke. *Archives of Physical Medicine and Rehabilitation* **77**: 707–9.

Tekeoolu Y, Adak B, Goksoy T (1998) Effect of transcutaneous electrical nerve stimulation (TENS) on Barthel Activities of Daily Living (ADL) index score following stroke. *Clinical Rehabilitation* **12**: 277–80.

Thaut MH, McIntosh GC, Rice RR (1997) Rhythmic facilitation of gait training in hemiparetic stroke rehabilitation. *Journal of Neurological Sciences* **151**: 207–12.

Theodorakis Y, Beneca A, Malliou P, Goudas M (1997) Examining psychological factors during injury rehabilitation. *Journal of Sport Rehabilitation* **6**: 355–63.

Toni D, Duca RD, Fiorelli M, *et al*, (1994) Pure motor hemiparesis and sensorimotor stroke: accuracy of very early clinical diagnosis of lacunar strokes. *Stroke* **25**: 92–6.

Towle D, Lincoln NB, Mayfield LM (1989) Service provision and functional independence in depressed stroke patients and the effect of social work intervention on these. *Journal of Neurology, Neurosurgery and Psychiatry* **52**: 519–22.

Tucker MA, Davidson JG, Ogle S (1984) Day hospital rehabilitation: effectiveness and cost in the elderly: a randomised controlled trial. *British Medical Journal* **289**: 1209–12.

Twomey C (1978) Brain tumours in the elderly. *Age and Ageing* **7**: 138–45.

Tyson SF, Ashburn A (1994) The influence of walking aids on hemiplegic gait. *Physiotherapy Theory and Practice* **10**: 77–86.

Tyson S, Thornton H, Downes A (1998) The effect of a hinged ankle-foot orthosis on hemiplegic gait: four single case studies. *Physiotherapy Theory and Practice* **14**: 75 –85.

Vallet G, Ahmaidi S, Serres I, *et al*, (1997) Comparison of two training programmes in chronic airway limitation patients: standardised versus individualised protocols. *European Respiratory Journal* **10**: 114–22.

van Vliet P, Sheridan M, Kerwin DG, Fentem P (1995) The influence of functional goals on the kinematics of reaching following stroke. *Neurology Report* **19**: 11–6.

Victor CR, Vetter NJ (1988) Preparing the elderly for discharge from hospital: a neglected aspect of patient care? *Age and Ageing* **17**: 155–63.

Visintin M, Barbeau H, Korner-Bitensky N, Mayo NE (1998) A new approach to retrain gait in stroke patients through body weight support and treadmill stimulation. *Stroke* **29**: 1122–8.

Visser MC, Koudstaal PJ, Erdman RAM, *et al*, (1995) Measuring quality of life in patients with myocardial infarction or stroke: a feasibility study of four questionnaires in The Netherlands. *Journal of Epidemiology and Community Health* **49**: 513–7.

Vissers MC, Hasman A, van der Linden CJ (1996) Impact of a protocol processing system (ProtoVIEW) on clinical behaviour of residents and treatment. International *Journal of Biomedical Computing* **42**: 143–50.

von Arbin M, Britton M, de Faire U, *et al*, (1981) Accuracy of bedside diagnosis of stroke. *Stroke* **12**: 288–93.

Wade DT (1996) Epidemiology of disabling neurological disease: how and why does disability occur? *Journal of Neurology, Neurosurgery and Psychiatry* **61**: 242–9.

Wade DT (1998a) Evidence relating to assessment in rehabilitation. *Clinical Rehabilitation* **12**: 183–6.

Wade DT (1998b) Evidence relating to goal planning in rehabilitation. *Clinical Rehabilitation* **12**: 273–5.

Wade DT (1999) Goal planning in stroke rehabilitation: how? *Topics in Stroke Rehabilitation* **6**: 16–36.

Wade DT, Langton Hewer R, Skilbeck CE, Bainton D, Burns-Cox C (1985a) Controlled trial of a home-care service for acute stroke patients. *Lancet*; **1**: 323–6.

Wade DT, Langton Hewer R (1985b) Hospital admission for acute stroke: who, for how long, and to what effect? *Journal of Epidemiology and Community Health* **39**: 347–52.

Wade DT, Legh-Smith J, Langton-Hewer R (1986) Effects of living with and looking after survivors of a stroke. *British Medical Journal* **293**: 418–20.

Wade DT, Collen FM, Robb GF, Warlow CP (1992) Physiotherapy intervention late after stroke and mobility. *British Medical Journal* **304**: 609–13.

Wagenaar RC, Meijer OG, van Wieringen PCW, *et al*, (1990) The functional recovery of stroke: a comparison between neuro-developmental treatment and the Brunnstrom method. *Scandinavian Journal of Rehabilitation Medicine* **22**: 1–8.

Waldron RM, Bohannon RW (1989) Weight distribution when standing: the influence of a single point cane in patients with stroke. *Physiotherapy Practice* **5**: 171–5.

Walker MF, Drummond AER, Lincoln NB (1996) Evaluation of dressing practice for stroke patients after discharge from hospital: a crossover design study. *Clinical Rehabilitation* **10**: 23–31.

Walker MF, Gladman JF, Lincoln NB, *et al*, (1999) Occupational therapy for stroke patients not admitted to hospital: a randomised controlled trial. *Lancet* **354**: 278–80.

Walker-Batson D, Smith P, Curtis S, *et al*, (1995) Amphetamine paired with physical therapy accelerates motor recovery after stroke: further evidence. *Stroke* **26**: 2254–9.

Wall JC, Turnbull GI (1987) Evaluation of out-patient physiotherapy and a home exercise program in the management of gait asymmetry in residual stroke. *Journal of Neurologic Rehabilitation* **1**: 115–23.

Wanklyn P, Forster A, Young J (1996) Hemiplegic shoulder pain (HSP): natural history and investigation of associated features. *Disability and Rehabilitation* **18**: 497–501.

Wannamethee SG, Shaper AG, Whincup PH, Walker M (1995) Smoking cessation and the risk of stroke in middle-aged men. *Journal of the American Medical Association* **274**: 155–60.

Wannamethee SG, Shaper AG, Walker M, Ebrahim S (1998) Lifestyle and 15 year survival free of heart attack, stroke and diabetes in middle-aged British men. *Archives of Internal Medicine* **158**: 2433–40.

Wardlaw JM, Yamaguchi T, del Zoppo G. (1996) Thrombolysis for acute ischaemic stroke. In: The Cochrane Library, Issue 3, Oxford; Update Software, 1999.

Warlow CP, Dennis MS, van Gijn J, Hankey GJ *et al*, (1996) Stroke: a practical guide to management. Blackwell Science.

Webb PM, Glueckauf RL (1994) The effects of direct involvement in goal setting on rehabilitation outcome for persons with traumatic brain injuries. *Rehabilitation Psychology* **39**: 179–88.

Webb DJ, Fayad PB, Wilbur C, *et al*, (1995) Effects of a specialised team on stroke care: the first two years of the Yale stroke program. *Stroke* **26**: 1353–7.

Wei F, Mark D, Hartz A, Campbell C (1995) Are PRO discharge screens associated with post-discharge adverse outcomes? *Health Services Research* **30**: 489–506.

Wells PS, Lensing AW, Hirsh J (1994) Graduated compression stockings in the prevention of postoperative venous thromboembolism: a meta-analysis. *Archives of Internal Medicine* **154**: 67–72.

Wellwood I, Dennis M, Warlow CP (1995) A comparison of the Barthel index and the OPCS instrument used to measure outcome after stroke. *Age and Ageing* **24**: 54–7.

Werner RA, Kessler S (1996) Effectiveness of an intensive outpatient rehabilitation program for postacute stroke patients. *American Journal of Physical Medicine and Rehabilitation* **75**: 114–20.

Wertz RT, Collins MJ, Weiss D, *et al*, (1981) Veterans Administration cooperative study on aphasia: a comparison of individual and group treatment. *Journal of Speech and Hearing Research* **24**: 580–94.

Wertz RT, Weiss DG, Aten JL, *et al*, (1986) Comparison of clinic, home and deferred language treatment for aphasia. *Archives of Neurology* **43**: 653–8.

West R, Stockel S (1965) The effect of meprobamate on recovery from aphasia. *Journal of Speech and Hearing Research* **8**: 57–62.

Whelton PK, Appel LJ, Espeland MA, *et al*, (1998) Sodium reduction and weight loss in the treatment of hypertension in older persons: a randomised controlled trial of non-pharmacologic interventions in the elderly (TONE). *Journal of the American Medical Association* **279**: 839–46.

Whurr R, Lorch MP, Nye C (1992) A meta-analysis of studies carried out between 1946 and 1988 concerned with the efficacy of speech and language therapy treatment for aphasic patients. *European Journal of Disorders of Communication* **27**: 1–18.

Wiffen P, McQuay H, Carroll D, *et al*, (1999) Anticonvulsant drugs for acute and chronic pain (Cochrane Review). In: The Cochrane Library, Issue 3, 1999. Oxford: Update Software.

Wikander B, Ekelund P, Milsom I (1998) An evaluation of multidisciplinary intervention governed by Functional Independence Measure (FIM) in incontinent stroke patients. *Scandinavian Journal of Rehabilitation Medicine* **30**: 15–21.

Williams A (1994) What bothers caregivers of stroke victims? *Journal of Neuroscience Nursing* **26**: 155–61.

Winchester P, Montgomery J, Bowman B, Hislop H (1983) Effects of feedback stimulation training and cyclical electrical stimulation on knee extension in hemiparetic patients. *Physical Therapy* **63**: 1096–103.

Winn C (1998) Complications with urinary catheters. *Professional Nurse Study Supplement* **13**: S7–S13.

Wolf SL, Catlin PA, Blanton S, *et al*, (1994) Overcoming limitations in elbow movement in the presence of antagonist hyperactivity. *Physical Therapy* **74**: 826–35.

Wong AM, Lee MY, Kuo JK, Tang FT (1997) The development and clinical evaluation of a standing biofeedback trainer. *Journal of Rehabilitation Research and Development* **34**: 322–7.

World Health Organisation (1978) Cerebrovascular disorders: a clinical and research classification. Geneva: WHO. Offset Publication No.43.

Yekutiel M, Guttman E (1993) A controlled trial of the retraining of the sensory function of the hand in stroke patients. *Journal of Neurology, Neurosurgery and Psychiatry* **56**: 241–4.

Young JB, Forster A (1992) The Bradford community stroke trial: results at six months. *British Medical Journal* **304**: 1085–9.

Young J, Forster A (1993) Day hospital and home physiotherapy for stroke patients: a comparative cost-effectiveness study. *J R Coll Physicians Lond* **27**: 252–8.

Young GR, Sandercock PAG, Slattery J, *et al*, (1996) Observer variation in the interpretation of intra-arterial angiograms and the risk of inappropriate decisions about carotid endarterectomy. *Journal of Neurology, Neurosurgery and Psychiatry* **60**: 152–7.

Appendix 1
Peer and utility reviews

A — Peer reviewers 1998 –99

Dietetics

Ms June Copeman	Leeds Metropolitan University
Mrs J Grigg	British Dietetic Association
Ms Norma McGough	British Diabetic Association
Ms Helen Molyneux	Dewsbury Healthcare NHS Trust
Ms Clare Murray	Worthing Hospital

General Practice

Royal College of General Practitioners Guidelines group

Medicine

Dr John Bamford	St James's University Hospital, Leeds
Dr Philip Bath	Nottingham City Hospital
Dr Richard Greenwood	National Hospital, Queen Square, London
Dr Richard Hardie	St George's Hospital, Tooting
Professor L Kalra	King's College School of Medicine, London
Professor Lindsy McLellan	Southampton General Hospital
Dr Ian Starke	Lewisham Hospital NHS Trust
Dr Pippa Tyrrell	Hope Hospital, Salford
Professor John Young	St Luke's Hospital, Bradford
Dr David Bowsher	The Pain Relief Foundation, Walton Hospital, Liverpool

Nursing

Professor Lorraine Smith	University of Glasgow
Clare Morrell	Clinical Effectiveness, Royal College of Nursing
Ms Liz Shirran	University of Aberdeen (Cochrane review Continence aids)
Sue Thomas	RCN Advisor on Disability and Chronic Disease
Nursing Rehabilitation Forum	**Royal College of Nursing**

Occupational Therapy

Annette Champion	Head of National Association of Neurological Occupational Therapists (**NANOT**)
Ms Christine Sealey	**College of Occupational Therapy**

Physiotherapy

(a) Chartered Society of Physiotherapy set up a Guidelines Support Group including representation from their specialist groups:

Ms A Archer	City & Hackney Community Services, for **ACPC***
Dr Ann Ashburn	Southampton General Hospital, for **ACPIN***
Mrs S Hogg	Queen Alexandra Hospital, Portsmouth, for **AGILE***
Mrs S Irani	Ealing Hospital, Southall, for **ACPIN**
Ms L Johnson	Airedale General Hospital, Keighley, for **AGILE**

(b) Peer review was also provided by:

Mrs Anthea Dendy	St George's Hospital, Tooting
Dr Anne Forster	St Luke's Hospital, Bradford
Dr Val Pomeroy	The Stroke Association Research Unit, Hope Hospital, Salford
Ms Judy Mead	Head of Clinical Effectiveness, **Chartered Society of Physiotherapy**

Psychology

Professor Nadina Lincoln	University of Nottingham
Professor Ian Robertson	Trinity College, Dublin

Radiology

	Royal College of Radiologists
Dr MD Hourihan	Consultant Neuroradiologist, University of Wales

Speech and Language Therapy

Dr Karen Bryan	University College Hospital, London
Mr Chris Eales	Action for Dysphasic Adults
Professor Pam Enderby	Centre for Ageing and Rehabilitation Studies, Sheffield
Ms Mandy LeMay	First Community Health NHS Trust, Cannock, Staffs
Ms Diana Moir	Camden & Islington Community Trust, London
Ms Charlotte Painter	**Action for Dysphasic Adults**
Ms Carole Pound	City University, London
Ms Debbie Rossiter	**Royal College of Speech & Language Therapy**
Ms Jenny Greener	University of Aberdeen (Cochrane reviews)

Surgery

Professor AD Mendelow	Consultant Neurosurgeon, University of Newcastle
Mr Mark Scriven	Consultant General & Vascular Surgeon, Wrexham Maelor Hospital
Ms Theresa von Goetz	Neurosurgical Registrar (interest in differential diagnosis in stroke)

*ACPC — Association of Chartered Physiotherapists in the Community
ACPIN — Association of Chartered Physiotherapists in Neurology
AGILE — Association of Chartered Physiotherapists in Elderly Care

B — Utility review 1999

A stratified sample of hospitals and trusts participating in the National Sentinel Audit of Stroke 1998 were sent the guidelines for utility review

Ipswich Hospital NHS Trust	Anglia & Oxford
Kettering General Hospital NHS Trust	Anglia & Oxford
Oxfordshire Community Health NHS Trust	Anglia & Oxford
Belfast City Hospital Health & Social Services Trust	Northern Ireland
Sperrin Lakeland Health & Social Care NHS Trust	Northern Ireland
Barnet and Chase Farm Hospitals NHS Trust (Barnet General Hospital site)	North Thames
Mid-Essex Hospital Services NHS Trust	North Thames
Mount Vernon & Watford Hospitals NHS Trust (Mount Vernon Hospital Site)	North Thames
Newham Healthcare NHS Trust	North Thames
Royal Free Hampstead NHS Trust	North Thames
University College London Hospitals NHS Trust	North Thames
Chorley & South Ribble NHS Trust	North West
Morecambe Bay Hospitals NHS Trust	North West
Southport and Ormskirk Hospital NHS Trust	North West
Stockport Acute Services NHS Trust	North West
Wirral & West Cheshire Community Health Care NHS Trust	North West
Bradford Hospitals NHS Trust	Northern & Yorkshire
Huddersfield NHS Trust	Northern & Yorkshire
North Durham Acute Hospitals NHS Trust	Northern & Yorkshire
Pinderfields & Pontefract Hospitals NHS Trust	Northern & Yorkshire
Royal Victoria Infirmary	Northern & Yorkshire
South Durham NHS Trust Darlington Memorial Hospital	Northern & Yorkshire
Bath & West Community NHS Trust	South & West
East Gloucestershire NHS Trust	South & West
North Bristol NHS Trust	South & West
Portsmouth Health Care NHS Trust	South & West
Royal United Hospital Bath NHS Trust	South & West
Wiltshire and Swindon Healthcare NHS Trust	South & West
Epsom Health Care NHS Trust	South Thames
Frimley Park Hospitals NHS Trust	South Thames
Richmond Twickenham & Roehampton Health Care NHS Trust	South Thames
Royal West Sussex Hospital	South Thames
Chesterfield and North Derbyshire Royal Hospital NHS Trust	Trent
Grantham & District Hospital NHS Trust	Trent
Leicester General Hospital NHS Trust	Trent
Llandough Hospital & Community NHS Trust	Wales
North Glamorgan NHS Trust	Wales
North West Wales NHS Trust	Wales
George Eliot Hospital NHS Trust	West Midlands

| Hereford Hospitals NHS Trust | West Midlands |
| Warwick Hospital NHS Trust | West Midlands |

Volunteers and others who participated in the utility review

Dr Joyce Abrahams, Whiston Hospital, Prescot, Merseyside

Ms Jane Barnacle, Therapy Service Manager, Royal Hampshire County Hospital, Winchester

Dr Rod Bland, Camborne and Redruth Hospital, Cornwall

Dr Nicola Brain, Consultant Physician in Rehabilitation Medicine, Walsgrave Hospital, Coventry

Dr RR Campbell, Consultant Physician, Princess Royal Hospital, Telford

Ms Carol Croser, Ward Manager Stroke Unit, York District Hospital

Dr Christine Davison, Consultant Physician, East Cheshire NHS Trust, Macclesfield

Dr Dewar, East Glamorgan County Hospital and Llwynypia Hospital

Dr A Dunn, Bronllys Hospital, Brecon, Powys

Dr Footit, Derriford Hospital, Plymouth

Mr Sanjay Gupta, Occupational Therapy Department, Greenwich District Hospital

Ms Sharon Hamilton, Senior Lecturer in Nursing & Research, St Helier Hospital, Carshalton

Dr C Hudson, Singleton Hospital, Sketty, Swansea

Dr HW Jones, Leighton Hospital, Crewe, Cheshire

Ms Julie Jones, Clinical Audit Department, Wrexham Medical Institute,

Dr P Jones, Ceredigion & Mid Wales NHS Trust, Bronglais Hospital, Aberystwyth

Dr Val Jones, Consultant Physician for Stroke, Mayday Hospital, Thornton Heath

Dr S Kar, Bassetlaw District General Hospital, Worksop

Dr Anne McEvoy, York Health Services NHS Trust

Ms Joan Melville, Plymouth Community Trust

Dr Jacintha Morgan, Cornwall Hospitals (Treliske)

Dr JR Naylor, Huddersfield Royal Infirmary

Dr K Niranjan, St George's Hospital, Ilford

Dr Steve Novak, Brighton General Hospital

Dr James Okwera, Stroke Physician, Rotherham District General Hospital

Mrs J Pawson, The Stroke Team, Briarfield, Nelson, Lancs

Dr Michael Power, The Ulster Community Hospitals Trust, Belfast

Dr Mark Roberts & Dr DP Davies, Cumberland Hospital, Carlisle Hospitals

Dr David Sandler, Arden Lodge (Stroke Unit), Birmingham Heartlands Hospital

Dr Martin Sandler, Solihull Stroke Unit, Chair of the Stroke Services Group

Dr C Sumanaya, Wolfson NeuroRehabilitation Unit, Atkinson Morley's Hospital

Dr Alan Thompson, National Hospital, Queen Square, London

Health Authorities

Nicky Hayworth, Clinical Effectiveness, Portsmouth and SE Hants Health Authority

Louise Ingram, Eastern Health & Social Services, Northern Ireland

Dr Jeremy White, Wakefield Health Authority

Miscellaneous

Rosalind Mitchell, Community Dental Service, Chesterfield

Appendix 2
List of national databases of research in progress

Research type	Organisation	Address	Database type & name	Web address
Health research covering varying aspects of stroke	NHS R&D programme	NHS R&D Programme on Cardiovascular Disease & Stroke, R&D Directorate, NHS Executive Northern & Yorkshire, Department of Health, John Snow House, Durham University Science Park, Durham DH1 3YG	Website: NHS R&D funded projects	www.doh.gov/nth&york/cvd
Medical	Medical Research Council	Medical Research Council 20 Park Crescent, London NW1N 4AL	Website: MRC funded projects database	www.mrc.ac.uk
Controlled trials	Medical Research Council	Medical Research Council 20 Park Crescent, London NW1N 4AL	Website: Controlled clinical trials database (in the process of development)	Link with Current Sciences internet site through www.controlled-trials.com
Therapy	*Collaboration of:* The Chartered Society of Physiotherapy College of Occupational Therapists Royal College of Speech & Language Therapy	Chartered Society of Physiotherapy 14 Bedford Row, London WC1R 4ED College of Occupational Therapists 106–114 Borough High Street Southwark, London SE1 1LB Royal College of Speech and Language Therapy, 7 Bath Place, Rivington St, London EC2A 3DR	CD-ROM: Register of therapy researchers version 2 1999	
Nursing	Royal College of Nursing	RCN Research & Development Co-ordinating Centre, School of Nursing, University of Manchester, Gateway House, Piccadilly, Manchester M60 7LP	Website: RCN Research & Development Co-ordinating Centre	www.man.ac.uk/rcn

Appendix 3
List of useful addresses

* Addresses suggested by patients with Stroke and their carers as particularly useful to them

Patients' and carers' organisations

Action for Dysphasic Adults*
Canterbury House
1 Royal Street
London SE1 7LL

Tel: 0171 261 9572

Benefits Enquiry Line*

Tel: 0800 882200

British Brain & Spine
Foundation*
7 Winchester House
Kennington Park
Cranmer Rd
London SW9 6EJ

Tel: 0171 793 5900

Carers National Association
20/25 Glasshouse Yard*
London EC1A 4JT

Tel: 0171 490 8818

College of Health*
21 Old Ford Road
London E2 9PL

Tel: 0181 983 1225
Fax: 0181 983 1553

Continence Foundation*
2 Doughty Street
London WC1

Tel: 0171 404 6875

Different Strokes*
Sir Walter Scott House
PO Box 5082
Milton Keynes MK5 7ZH

Tel: 01908 236033

SPOD*
(Association to aid the Sexual
and Personal Relationships of
People with a Disability)
286 Camden Road
London N7 0BJ

Tel: 0171 607 8851

Stroke Associations

Chest Heart & Stroke, Scotland*
65 North Castle Street
Edinburgh EH2 3LT

Tel: 0131 225 6963

Northern Ireland Chest Heart &
Stroke Association*
21 Dublin Road
Belfast BT2 7HB

Tel:01232 327040

The Stroke Association*
Stroke House
Whitecross Street
London EC1Y 8JJ

Tel: 0171 566 0300

Driving License Authority

Drivers' Medical Branch
DVLA
Swansea SA99 1TU
(For medical advisors and
literature
Tel: 01792 783686)

Professional bodies

Chartered Society of
Physiotherapy
14 Bedford Row
London WC1R 4ED

Tel: 0171 306 6666

College of Occupational
Therapists
106–114 Borough High Street
Southwark
London SE1 1LB

Tel: 0171 357 6480

Royal College of Nursing
20 Cavendish Square
London W1M 0AB

Tel: 0171 409 3333

Royal College of Physicians
11 St Andrews Place
London NW1 4LE

Tel: 0171 935 1174

Royal College of Speech &
Language Therapy
7 Bath Place
Rivington St
London EC2A 3DR

Tel: 0171 613 3855

Index